DOUG K. REED

TEN MEN

THE RICH CONNECTIONS EVERY MAN NEEDS

A STUDY OF KING DAVID

Unless otherwise indicated, all Scripture quotations are taken from the *Holy Bible, New Living Translation*, © 1996, 2004, 2007 by Tyndale House Foundation. Used by permission of Tyndale House Publishers, Inc., Carol Stream, Illinois 60188. All rights reserved. Scripture quotations marked (NIV) are taken from the *Holy Bible, New International Version*®, NIV®, © 1973, 1978, 1984, 2011 by Biblica, Inc.® Used by permission of Zondervan. All rights reserved worldwide. www.zondervan.com. The "NIV" and "New International Version" are trademarks registered in the United States Patent and Trademark Office by Biblica, Inc.® Scripture quotations marked (AMP) are taken from *The Amplified® Bible*, © 2015 by The Lockman Foundation, La Habra, CA. Used by permission. (www.Lockman.org). Scripture quotations marked (AMPC) are taken from the *Amplified® Bible* Copyright © 1954, 1958, 1962, 1964, 1965, 1987 by The Lockman Foundation Used by permission. lockman.org. All rights reserved. Scripture quotations marked (KJV) are taken from the King James Version of the Holy Bible. Scripture quotations marked (NKJV) are taken from the *New King James Version*, © 1979, 1980, 1982 by Thomas Nelson, Inc. Used by permission. All rights reserved. Scripture quotations marked (MSG) are taken from *The Message: The Bible in Contemporary Language* by Eugene H. Peterson, © 1993, 1994, 1995, 1996, 2000, 2001, 2002. Used by permission of NavPress Publishing Group. All rights reserved. Represented by Tyndale House Publishers, Inc. Scripture quotations marked (ESV) are taken from *The Holy Bible, English Standard Version*, © 2016, 2000, 2001, 1995 by Crossway Bibles, a division of Good News Publishers. Used by permission. All rights reserved. Scripture quotations marked (TLB) are taken from *The Living Bible*, © 1971. Used by permission of Tyndale House Publishers, Inc., Carol Stream, Illinois 60188. All rights reserved. Scripture quotations noted (CEB) are taken from the Common English Bible, copyright 2011. Used by permission. All rights reserved. Scripture quotations marked (NLV) are taken from the *New Life Version*, Copyright © 1969 and 2003. Used by permission of Barbour Publishing, Inc., Uhrichsville, Ohio 44683. All rights reserved. Scripture quotations taken from the (NASB®) *New American Standard Bible*®, Copyright © 1960, 1971, 1977, 1995, 2020 by The Lockman Foundation. Used by permission. All rights reserved. lockman.org. Scripture quotations taken from the New Century Version® (NCV). Copyright © 2005 by Thomas Nelson. Used by permission. All rights reserved. Scripture quotations taken from the *Modern English Version* (MEV). Copyright © 2014 by Military Bible Association. Used by permission. All rights reserved.

Boldface type in the Scripture quotations indicates the author's emphasis.

TEN MEN
The Rich Connections Every Man Needs (A Study of King David)

Doug Reed
Partnership International
www.pitrips.com
www.dougkreed.com

ISBN: 979-8-88769-344-6 • eBook ISBN: 979-8-88769-345-3
Printed in the United States of America
© 2024 by Doug K. Reed

Whitaker House • 1030 Hunt Valley Circle • New Kensington, PA 15068
www.whitakerhouse.com

Library of Congress Control Number: 2024923665

No part of this book may be reproduced or transmitted in any form or by any means, electronic or mechanical—including photocopying, recording, or by any information storage and retrieval system—without permission in writing from the publisher. Please direct your inquiries to permissionseditor@whitakerhouse.com.

CONTENTS

Foreword by Darryl Strawberry 7
Introduction: The King's Advantage
(The Power of Relationships) 9
1. Spiritual Fathers (David & Samuel) 25
2. Ordained Opposition (David & Goliath, Saul) 41
3. Covenant Friendships (David & Jonathan) 61
4. Warrior Brothers (David & His Mighty Men) 79
5. Brave Partners (David & Abishai) 97
6. Spiritual Sons (David & Mephibosheth) 115
7. Powerful Prophets (David & Nathan) 135
8. Mighty Mentors (David & Joab) 155
9. Elite Forces (David & the Thirty-Three) 175
10. God's Heart (Becoming a Man who Chases
    the Heart of God) 195
Conclusion: The "Perfect Ten" Myth 215
About the Author 223

FOREWORD

This book isn't just another guide—it's a rallying cry, a call to arms for men everywhere who dare to live a life of purpose, courage, and deep connection. We stand at a crossroads in a world that celebrates rugged individualism and often shames vulnerability. Will we continue to isolate ourselves, convinced that strength is found in solitude? Or will we embrace the ancient wisdom that true power lies in brotherhood, shared battles, and lifting each other toward greatness?

The story of King David teaches us that even the mightiest warriors, the most revered leaders, are only as strong as the men they surround themselves with. David's life wasn't defined by the size of his kingdom or the number of victories but by the relationships that forged his character and fueled his mission. From Jonathan's steadfast loyalty to Nathan's courageous counsel, David thrived because he sought out and nurtured the right connections.

In *Ten Men: The Rich Connections Every Man Needs*, Doug K. Reed lays bare the truth: No man is an island, and no battle is won alone. This book will guide you through the sacred terrain of male relationships—mentors, friends, allies—and challenge you to find your tribe of "ten." Whether amid your Goliath-sized challenge or standing in the shadows waiting for your moment, these pages will awaken the warrior within you.

Let this book inspire you to lean into vulnerability, fight for connection, and build an eternal legacy of brotherhood. The battles ahead will not be easy, but with your tribe by your side, they will be worth it.

—*Darryl Strawberry*
Evangelist and four-time World Series champion

INTRODUCTION:
THE KING'S ADVANTAGE
(THE POWER OF RELATIONSHIPS)

A person standing alone can be attacked and defeated, but two can stand back-to-back and conquer. Three are even better, for a triple-braided cord is not easily broken.
—Ecclesiastes 4:12

David was the greatest earthly king ever to live. His unparalleled military victories, national unification efforts, massive building projects, and extraordinary spiritual leadership are just a few of his impressive accomplishments. David was a flawed and sinful man. However, God's hand was on David's life, ushering him to his destiny—even his failures seemed to propel him forward. But it was not his brilliance or giftedness that carried him to heights known by few men. What was the key to David's success? No one succeeds at the level David did by themselves. David's advantage, the king's advantage, was in the flourishing relationships he pursued and nurtured. This kingly advantage is available to you and me. It is the key to tremendous success and an extraordinary life beyond our imagination.

I own a short-term, project-based missions organization called Partnership International. We go into some of the poorest places in the world and execute meaningful building projects. Although it is rewarding, it is also incredibly challenging. The projects are only getting bigger, more expensive, and more complicated. But I have an advantage—a kingly advantage. I have spent the last thirty years building strategic kingdom-based relationships. I never go into a battle by myself. I have partners and warriors who go with me. We are blessed to take hundreds of people on our difference-making trips. I am thankful for the many friends and partners who have shared their wealth of skills and resources to enhance the lives of strangers. Together, we have achieved significant accomplishments that were once only dreams.

I am convinced that the devil, the enemy of our souls, is not afraid of any individual. Men often believe they are intimidating, but, alone, they lack the impact they imagine. However, a powerful "spiritual multiplication" is activated when men fight alongside each other. Deuteronomy 32:30 says, *"How could one chase a thousand, and two put ten thousand to flight…?"* (AMP). This is a good question because the equation does not make sense. If one can conquer a thousand, then two should be able to defeat two thousand. That is good arithmetic, right? Not according to God's calculations! He has keys on His calculator we do not have. According to God, the multiplication effect is miraculous when we get together. Our enemies are never intimidated when we are alone, but our togetherness and connection are the King's advantage!

God built you for connection. Your relational life is what will lead you to destiny and success. I encourage you to stop praying for resources and opportunities and begin praying for God-ordained relationships. You are only one key friendship away from treasure—a few relationships away from striking oil! You are not seeking people for blessing's sake but because you obey God's will. The kingdom of God is built on relationships, and God's primary way of blessing your life is through divine connections. I wrote *Ten Men* to help you define and find your God-given tribe. Life is not so much about *what* you are called to do; it's about *whom* you are called to do it with.

Next to Jesus, David might be the most relational person in the entire Bible. We have sixty-six chapters dedicated to his story (over fifty more than any other biblical character). They are all a raw record of human interaction on various levels. I chose him as a general and chronological study for male relationships because of his unique kinship with other men. David's masculine connections are a big part of what made him a fierce warrior and an outstanding leader. These divine connections were such an advantage to him that the enemies he faced never went up against just David. If you challenged this man, you would find him surrounded by a network of devoted friends and companions interconnected to his royal calling. David's example was not perfect, but it was always authentic. God placed this beautiful illustration of a highly relational man in Scripture for a reason. Together, we will discover why.

An old woodsman's proverb says, "A tree is best measured when it is down." How true this is when it comes to evaluating a legacy. Looking back on David, we have the unfair edge of hindsight and the unvarnished perspective of Scripture as we peer into his life. We will encounter a man with a mission so grand that he never could have accomplished it on his own. David intimately understood his need for others, whether from sheer self-awareness or desperation. Most men lack this simple but life-changing realization. We are not "desperados out riding fences" or "Supermen" with such great powers that no one could ever understand our burden. No, we are fragile creatures with destinies far beyond our finite abilities. All of us have giant weaknesses. We need help. We need each other.

FINDING TEN

In a traditional funeral, six to eight pallbearers will transport the casket. The word "pall" traces back to the Roman Empire, when the cape or cloak of a fallen warrior would be placed over the top of his body or casket. A modern-day equivalent would be a flag draped over the casket of a fallen soldier.[1]

When you carry the casket of someone, you are walking with the settled burdens of the completed battles they fought. But in that sacred moment, only a finished fight is acknowledged. You can't be in the battle with them because their war is over. Their conflicts have concluded. Eventually, all of us (symbolically or literally) will be carried to our graves by other people. They will support our bodies but not feel the weight of our burdens. While we live, we must not delay connecting with other men. Men are in relational crisis, and with this book, I am sounding the alarm to alert the hearts, minds, and souls of every man who dares to read it.

---

1. "The History Behind Pallbearers," Funeral Basics, accessed December 13, 2024, https://www.funeralbasics.org/the-history-behind-pallbearers.

My challenge is finding six to eight—or how about ten?—men to walk alongside you. We must learn to carry the burdens of each other's battles. Why wait for the casket to be lifted by the strength of others? Men should experience the beautiful camaraderie gained by sharing life instead of wallowing in the prison of seclusion. I meet men every day who crave connection. We hide our hunger with a shell of self-reliance, but the person hidden inside is starving for meaningful relationships. God placed in every man a sacred relational instinct, a holy impulse that refuses to allow the marriage of loneliness and contentment. The prison system has shown that solitary confinement is one of the worst punishments a prisoner can face. The extreme isolation magnifies the effect of their imprisonment—it is a form of torture. Freedom isn't freedom if you are living a chosen lifestyle of aloneness.

In her revolutionary book *Find Your People*, author Jennie Allen discovered through extensive research that the average person can only manage a network of about 150 relationships. These are mostly just connections, not close friendships. Most of us can only manage about fifty what we call "acquaintances" and only fifteen real friendships. In fact, among those fifteen, you will have about five close friends.[2] These numbers average out to exactly *ten* significant relationships. In this book, I break those ten into specific relational categories essential in every man's life. We see all of them on display throughout David's life.

I see several advantageous qualities in David that helped him find his ten men:

---

2. Jennie Allen, *Find Your People: Building Deep Community in a Lonely World* (Colorado Springs, CO: WaterBrook, 2022), 8.

DAVID PASSIONATELY PURSUED HIS DESTINY.

The greatest way to befriend other warriors is to be engaged in a meaningful war. It's the difference between someone who would like to be friends with a drummer and a guitar player and the guy who starts a band and books a gig. People are drawn to a man who is actively living out his calling. When God gave me the outline for this book, and I studied the categories, I was amazed at the extensive collection of deep relationships God has allowed me to experience. How did it happen? In living life, pursuing my destiny, and engaging in my battles, I found the relationships I needed. Never be the guy sitting around wishing he had friends or partners. Pursue your calling, engage in your God-given destiny, and others will be drawn to you. You will find *whom* you are looking for as you go after *what* God has for you. The Holy Spirit has a way of cross-connecting your mission with the right people when you are actively living out His plans.

DAVID GAVE CONSISTENT, INTENTIONAL INVITATIONS FOR OTHERS TO JOIN HIM.

With all the pain and betrayal he experienced, it would have been easy for David to insulate and isolate himself, but we observe the opposite. From his most significant successes to his darkest hours, we see a God-ordained king who refuses to lead alone. David's openness to relationships was both selective and adventurous. He was willing to let others in, even when it could harm himself or his position. David knew that his need for connection was worth navigating the inherent dangers. This is a courageous trait that every man needs to possess. We should always place a welcome sign at the door of our lives, even though some will probably abuse the privilege. Far too many of us have sequestered ourselves in a feeble attempt at self-preservation.

A few years ago, I taught an evening Bible study for men on a weekly basis. The group grew to approximately sixty guys, not because of my teaching but because of the fantastic camaraderie and fellowship. One day at church, I invited a man who seemed interested in the study to join us. He seemed ready to commit to attending, but then he asked me, "Will I have to talk and share with other guys?" I told him there were table discussions after the teaching, which was the best part of the night. He quickly and firmly replied, "I'm out." I tried to discuss it further, but he would not budge. The prospect of connecting with other men killed the deal. I remember him acting like he was a "real man" because of his choice to isolate himself and avoid any risk of vulnerability. He was being very "un-David-like" because David was consistently willing to be vulnerable. The false lie of masculinity that far too many men tell themselves is that emotional detachment and numbness are acceptable. They fail to realize that there is nothing courageous about denying themselves the chance to know others and to be known. David's life is a brave example of someone who ultimately had the resources to avoid vulnerability—but he beautifully chose the opposite.

DAVID'S HUMILITY WAS ONE OF HIS MOST SIGNIFICANT RELATIONAL TRAITS.

David's story bleeds humility—from his unwillingness to promote himself to his honor for those above and below him. After his failures, David humbly received corrective voices to guide him back to right standing with God. He displayed meekness in his interactions. David's humility attracted the people he needed, which is what humility does. Pride repels; humility attracts. My pastor says, "Your strengths give you a role, but your weaknesses give you a team." I love that. Your humble expression of strength and honest admission of weakness attract the right people to your life. People want to know the real you. Humility creates relatability. Pride closes you in; humility opens you up.

> God goes against the willful proud; God gives grace to the willing humble.
>
> (James 4:6 MSG)

RELATIONAL RESPONSIBILITY

I have a dear friend named Pastor Marc who was born in Zimbabwe and raised in Botswana. Through a series of circumstances, God brought Pastor Marc to the United States, and he has become one of my favorite people to talk to about spiritual topics. Recently, we discussed an African term called *Ubuntu*. Pastor Marc passionately explained that this term is a Zulu word that means, "We do not exist alone—we are all connected intricately." He even illustrated his point by talking about the division of human cells. Cells divide, but they are forever connected to the former cell. Like this, we are all a division of many others. Our origins are spiritually and relationally connected to other people. Pastor Marc spoke about how his ministry calling was now intertwined with the pastor under whom we both serve. He said, "Callings require connections." This statement is so true, not just for ministers but for every person.

This conversation intrigued me so much that I researched Ubuntu even further. This philosophy was a deep part of African culture, far beyond its place of origination. It loosely means "I am because we are." Ubuntu is often defined as "I am a person because of other people."[3] In other words, if I do not become who I am supposed to be, then the people I am supposed to connect with cannot become who they are supposed to be. No one lives

---

3. "Ubuntu – I am because you are," AFN 2020 Online, accessed December 13, 2024, https://www.afnconference.org.au/ubuntu-i-am-because-you-are.

on an island without consequence—we are relationally responsible to each other. Bill Clinton and Barack Obama, former presidents of the United States, and the late Nelson Mandela, former president of South Africa and anti-apartheid activist, used the concept of Ubuntu in their speeches. Sometimes, leaders will reference the idea to highlight community and living for causes bigger than yourself. That's great, but occasionally, powerful mantras are diluted when applied too broadly. "Ubuntu" is about our relationships. I have a fundamental responsibility to be the man God intends me to be so I can influence (consciously or unconsciously) other men. If I fail in my responsibility, that failure extends to every person I connect with.

I have experienced a living tapestry of kingdom connections. My relationships have been a big part of God's miracle of redemption in my life. Early in my walk with God, He spoke to me about "growing and connecting." He told me that if I grew, my ministry would grow, and that His kingdom was built on relationships. The Holy Spirit made me realize that my personal growth was not just "personal." If I refused to grow, I would have nothing to give to others. If I did not have meaningful relationships, I would not be connected to kingdom things. God's kingdom is not made of money and buildings—it is made of people. These kingdom principles are far removed from the way most men think.

We hear it all the time:

"You live your life, and I will live mine."

"You do you."

"I just want to be left alone."

It is as if somehow we can live individually without affecting each other collectively. We cannot live as if there is no "Ubuntu" between us! Everything I am and do creates a ripple that carries my impact into other people's lives. This is how the kingdom works.

I will talk more about David in a minute, but the greatest example of someone who lived in a way that recognized his relational responsibility was Jesus. Jesus was all that the Father meant for Him to be, which means we can become all God has intended for us to be through Him. In Christ, we have next-level "Ubuntu." In Him, there is relational perfection. Paul gave us this encouragement in Philippians 2:

> *In your relationships with one another, have the same mindset as Christ Jesus: Who, being in very nature God, did not consider equality with God something to be used to his own advantage; rather, he made himself nothing by taking the very nature of a servant, being made in human likeness. And being found in appearance as a man, he humbled himself by becoming obedient to death—even death on a cross!*
> (Philippians 2:5–8 NIV)

Jesus did not refuse the responsibility of the cross because He knew the cross connected Him to us. Without the humility of His sacrifice, a canyon of sin would still separate us from God. The cross was the most relational act to ever take place.

Jesus said, "*This is My commandment, that you love one another as I have loved you. Greater love has no one than this, than to lay down one's life for his friends*" (John 15:12–13 NKJV). What if we men led that way and began to lay our lives down with something other than personal success in mind? What if we realized that everything we do either adds to our collective "Ubuntu" or increases the tragic isolation that is overtaking so many of us? We would experience a game-changing shift in our communities. If my friend Pastor Marc could visit you personally, he would say, "Man of God, you need other men of God in your life." He would call out the "Ubuntu" inside of you. How many more men do we have to lose to the tragedy of suicide or just the slow death of detachment? We must stop the insanity and choose one another. Jesus did, and so did David.

Everywhere you look in David's story, you see him with other men. David was a gatherer who refused to do life alone. His battles were always fought with brothers by his side. His victories were always celebrated with the people who had helped him succeed. His table was filled with men ahead of him in character and many others who were his proteges. Relationships surrounded David. Even when someone betrayed him, David never wavered in his relational resolve. This was the king's advantage, and he used it until his dying day. Unlike most men, David seemed to know that his life was more significant than his needs or successes. David took delight in his relationships. He knew the joy of brotherhood and embraced the sting of a loving rebuke. This king was connected, and it was the foundation of everything he accomplished.

QUALITY CONTROL

Most of the men I know are not fans of crowds. They may like the excitement of a ball game or the spiritual energy of an excellent church service, but they would rather avoid crowds. I understand just how they feel! You can have your theme parks and your crowded interstates. I will take a serene lake or a secluded beach any day. But I don't want to be alone. If the crowds I encounter are a part of my mission, sign me up. Even then, I must take some friends with me. I cannot face the crowds alone.

Numbers are a funny thing, especially if you are a leader. We leaders always want more sales for our companies, but "more" means crowded stores and probably a depersonalized experience. Your food may be so good that you should open a chain of restaurants. How do you maintain quality when more personnel are needed? As a pastor, I want all the churches I work with to explode with growth. But filling seats on Sundays is not the same as discipleship. Take it from me: you can speak to thousands, but only a few will enrich your life. How many meaningful relationships will you have? The fellowship of the few will determine your life's quality and impact.

In David's life, we see a pattern. His big moments were usually followed by an expansion of his relationships. David never avoided crowded places that were connected to his purpose. But these extraordinary events were always followed by a seemingly ordinary fellowship with a few key people. Some of David's relationships were seasonal. In the same way, we need different people at different times. Others were a constant, steady force who supported him in life and his mission. David had both "lifers" and "lifters." Some stayed with him on his journey to the end, and others were only meant to carry him for a while. The key for King David, in the present and the future, was to have an inner circle with exclusive access to him. Everyone needs that.

We even see David employing the relational equivalent of special forces in his life (I will cover this topic in greater detail later on). A few select individuals fought the most brutal battles alongside him, experienced his most difficult moments, and shared his most memorable events. These advanced warriors helped David move forward when no one else could. We all need warriors.

According to the Bible, the *quality* of an army matters, not its size. We see this on full display in the story of Gideon in Judges 7. Gideon is an unlikely leader of Israel who was given an impossible task—defeating the vast Midianite army. The Midianite forces were *"like a swarm of locusts. Their camels were like grains of sand on the seashore—too many to count"* (Judges 7:12). Yet God told Gideon that he had too many men! He started with 22,000, and by the time God was done testing them, Gideon was left with a force of only 300 warriors. (See Judges 7:1–15.) God made Gideon undergo quality-control testing to ensure he had the right men. This testing is an essential practice for all of us. Not everybody is called. God has a select group of people with whom you are supposed to go into battle. By the end of Gideon's story, there is a God-given victory by a far superior force, albeit a small one. Can you imagine the camaraderie among the 300 after a victory like that? The depth of friendship that existed? What magnificent exclusivity it was to be a part of the fellowship of those few. God wants that for you. He has both your battle and your brothers already planned out. Will you be one of the few?

Jesus elaborated on this principle, saying, *"If two of you agree here on earth concerning anything you ask, my Father in heaven will do it for you. For where two or three gather together as my followers, I am there among them"* (Matthew 18:19–20). I love this verse in *The Living Bible* translation:

> *For where two or three gather together because they are mine, I will be right there among them.*
>
> (Matthew 18:20 TLB)

Did you catch those truths? We think that a miracle takes prayer from thousands of people, but Jesus said it takes just two.

It is not the vastness of your network that matters; it is the vitality of your agreement that makes the difference. Maybe two or three are the most potent quantities in the universe. But this kind of gathering only works when we are unified in Him. It is this unique and powerful fellowship God wants for you.

Have you ever tried to have fellowship among a disconnected crowd? Have you ever gone to dinner with dozens and left full of more than just food and drink? We should seek to form intimate connections among a select few. So, why not decide today that you will gather your two or three—or even as many as *ten*? You could start a movement and help others discover their select few.

LEADERS FIRST

Leaders direct, command, manage, and forge paths. They are the ones who should exhibit authenticity, integrity, and determination. However, I believe that leaders are not always the most gifted, called, connected, or charismatic.

One of the churches where I serve is located in the Tri-Cities area of Virginia. It is a large, vibrant church led by a highly gifted and anointed couple. Their giftedness and anointing are not what made them our leaders, but rather their unhesitating obedience to God to plant a church in a forgotten area. They went first, and the congregation followed as a harvest of the seeds they planted.

I often think about the first person who attempted to skydive or the first individual to deep-sea dive. They may have been brave, reckless, or perhaps a mix of both, but you cannot deny that they were a leader because they took the initiative to go first. That is what leaders do: leaders go first. God is calling some of us to be leaders for the first time. Will you jump into the unknown? Will you swim into the darkness of the deep? Or will you wait in safety while someone else goes first?

I have developed an addiction to watching surfing documentaries despite having grown up in Illinois. I am fascinated by these adventurers who take a wave as a "dare from God" and try to conquer it. One of my favorite stories is about a man named Phil Edwards. He was born in 1938 and grew up surfing the big waves off the Northern California coast. The giant waves ridden today would have been unfamiliar to surfers in the 50s. The most significant wave of his time was called "Killer Dana" off of Dana Point, California.[4] On a morning in 1953, Phil Edwards went first.[5] When he paddled out that day, I am sure he had no idea he was about to give birth to the sport we now know as performance surfing. He left the shores of safety, and many others followed his lead. Phil was known for talking about "the legions of the unjazzed"—those poor souls who would never know what it meant to take a risk and go first.

This book's "big wave" is for men like you and me to take the initiative and invite a generation to paddle out into new territory. I believe it will be the ride of our lives! Scary waters are where you find sunken treasures. Primitive artifacts of tried-and-true, ancient ways of doing life are waiting to be pulled to the surface by a leader like you. Someone must take the initiative; someone must go first. Maybe what you have always called "shyness" or insecurity is a fear that needs to be defeated. Perhaps that "loner" title you embraced was never given to you

---

4. Luís MP, "Phil Edwards: the first surfer of Pipeline," *SurferToday.com*, https://www.surfertoday.com/surfing/phil-edwards-the-first-surfer-of-pipeline#google_vignette.
5. Jason Borte, "Phil Edwards: Biography and Photos," *Surfline.com*, https://www.surfline.com/surf-news/phil-edwards/89812.

by God. Maybe your aversion to being close to others is scar tissue from past wounds. With a bit of training, you could lead your legion of godly men into the battles you are called to fight together. You could be the answer to the prayers of the lonely, and your reward could be even greater than theirs! It's your turn to go first.

1

SPIRITUAL FATHERS (DAVID & SAMUEL)

> *Samuel took his flask of oil and anointed him, with his brothers standing around watching. The Spirit of G*OD *entered David like a rush of wind, God vitally empowering him for the rest of his life.*
> —1 Samuel 16:13 (MSG)

I'm a fan of old Western movies, especially those featuring John Wayne. One of my favorites is *The Cowboys*, in which he plays an older cattle herder who must drive his cattle to market but can't find capable men to help. Instead, he mentors ten boys, ages thirteen to seventeen, teaching them to ride, rope, and shoot while becoming a father figure to them.

The boys each grapple with personal issues, and as they journey together, Wayne helps them navigate their fears and anger. The movie reaches a climax when rustlers invade their camp. Wayne, despite his age and injuries, confronts the lead rustler, only to be shot and left to die after a fierce fight. In his final moments, he urges the boys to "be men" and aspire to be better than him.

After his death, the boys rise to the occasion, tying up the cook, arming themselves, and using their learned skills to defeat the rustlers and reclaim the cattle. The scene where they ride into the market as transformed young men is powerful. It's a reminder of the importance of mentorship and how spiritual fathers can inspire growth and courage. What a film. They don't make them like that anymore, but perhaps they can again.

The issue of fatherlessness is a two-sided coin. There is both a need to be and a need to receive. You may be reading this book and thinking, "Man, I really need a father." You long to have someone guide you and call out the man you are meant to be. The other side of the fatherless coin is the need for spiritual dads. Everyone knows someone over whom he has influence. No matter how messed up you think you are, you are doing better than someone. Even your areas of defeat can provide a place of authentic relatability and create a platform of meaningful mentorship. Fathers play a prophetic role that is deeper than mentoring. Fathers can awaken destinies and prophesy the future. The father's voice is one of the most powerful things in the universe. God is calling His men to find their father voice.

Fatherhood and motherhood are vastly different occupations. I would never debate with a mom about who loves their kids more. Moms will always win that argument! Men can't compete with carrying a living being for nine months and then giving birth. I am convinced that if I lost an arm in a chainsaw accident, although my wife would be compassionate, in the back of her mind, she would be thinking, "It's not as if you gave birth!" My wife loves our kids so much that she would do anything for them. She would use skills like a superheroine or stuntwoman to ensure their safety. She has no hesitation; most of the time, her love outpaces mine. However, her voice is not as powerful as the voice God gave me. My father voice carries a certain weight that hers is not designed to carry. God has ordained the voice of a father to call out the future in the next generation. This profound influence can be used for healing or for harm. Being a father (literally or spiritually) is one of the most significant responsibilities on earth.

FATHERLY VISION

Samuel, a powerful priest and prophet, was on a God-mandated mission. God had rejected Saul as king of Israel. (See 1 Samuel 15:26–28.) God told Samuel about Jesse, who lived near Bethlehem in the rugged Judean hills, because He had chosen one of Jesse's sons to be the next king of Israel. Although he feared King Saul, Samuel obeyed God and headed toward Bethlehem. Jesse had seven sons walk before Samuel, but God told Samuel that none of these impressive young men was the one He had chosen.

The most astounding part of this scene in 1 Samuel 16:12–13 is what is missing. David's father thought so little of him that he did not invite him to the most significant moment in their family's history. The clear inference is that Jesse could not or would not see David's potential. He thought David was only good for taking care of the sheep.

GOD HAS ORDAINED THE VOICE
OF A FATHER TO CALL OUT
THE FUTURE IN THE NEXT
GENERATION.

> Then Samuel asked, "Are these all the sons you have?" "There is still the youngest," Jesse replied. "But he's out in the fields watching the sheep and goats." "Send for him at once," Samuel said. "We will not sit down to eat until he arrives." (1 Samuel 16:11)

Did you catch that last line? Samuel felt divine providence was at hand when he heard about Jesse's eighth son. He stood up for David before even meeting him.

Fathers are supposed to have vision. Fathers are gifted to see the hidden potential in their sons and daughters before anyone else does. I knew the calling and potential of each of my three kids well ahead of them. This advanced knowledge is the proper order between fathers and their children. When fathers are blinded, like Jesse was, a spiritual sequence is broken, creating a wandering soul. Fathers are to lift confusion and bring clarity, but absentee fathers do the opposite. Could David have failed Jesse in some way and lost his confidence? In verse 11, Jesse calls him *"the youngest,"* the one *"watching the sheep and goats."* In *The Message* translation, it uses the term *"the runt."* Jesse had categorized David as the least among his sons. Jesse broke the spiritual order, and in this providential moment, a spiritual father named Samuel stepped in. Someone needed to see what David's father could not.

Have you ever had your image frozen in time by someone who used to know you? It could have been an old college roommate thinking you would be the same immature prankster you were in college. Or it could have been someone as close as a father who refused to see past your momentary failures, so he created an image of you that left you stuck in an unchangeable past. I think this is what happened between Jesse and David. It could have been a childish screw-up on David's part that made his father freeze him in time, so to speak. After all, Jesse had seven other sons, so there was no need to give David any of his precious mental energy. This kind of thinking is such a problem in relationships! A singular judgment based on an out-of-date history can trap someone in their past, no matter how much they have grown. Our lives are not snapshots—they are movie reels. We are constantly moving and growing.

Why not start giving "the gift of a spiritual update"? It is one of the spiritual disciplines I try to practice. Ask God to "update your operating system" toward others; it will widen your relational pool by miles. Without this practice, we risk being like Jesse, never becoming the "Samuels" our world desperately needs. We need to keep in mind that love *"keeps no record of wrongs"* (1 Corinthians 13:5 NIV).

I love verse thirteen of our text! *"So as David stood there among his brothers, Samuel took the flask of olive oil he had brought and anointed David with the oil. And the Spirit of the LORD came powerfully upon David from that day on"* (1 Samuel 16:13). A fatherly prophet saw what others couldn't and was used by God in a way they never could've been. Samuel anointed the next king of Israel. He called forth a future out of David that even David was unaware of. This moment would mark David for the rest of his life.

Every man longs for someone to do what Samuel did—for a father to call out the best in him and to see what only God can reveal. By his actions, Samuel whispered in the ear of an unknowing David, "You will be the next king of Israel." He saw what no one could see, so he got to say what no one else could. Samuel spoke into David's royal destiny, and David would never recover. Samuel did what fathers are supposed to do.

THE FATHER VOICE

We do not have an extensive record of the conversations between David and Samuel. We know that after Saul began attacking him, David went to Samuel in Ramah and told him all that Saul had done. Samuel kept David with him and protected him there in Naioth in Ramah. (See 1 Samuel 19:18.) I wish we could hear the talks that took place between David and his spiritual father. One can only imagine the deep wisdom the aged prophet shared. Did he speak to David's gifts? Did his words heal the wounds inflicted by David's father, Jesse? Did he teach David how to be a king? If God wanted us to know, He would have placed it in the text for all to see. We know that David needed someone to see and say what his father would not or could not. Samuel stood in that role, even for only a moment. All it takes is one encounter with a spiritual father to change your life and launch you toward your future. David would experience other voices, but his time with Samuel, however brief it was, was the catalyst for all that God would do through him. This is the power of the father voice.

One of my fondest memories of using my father voice was with my son, Jordan, when he was around thirteen years of age. I grew up hunting deer with my dad. It is a generational skill that he passed down to my brother and me. I decided I would do the same for my son. After a few exploratory trips to a property where I had obtained permission to hunt, the big morning came, and I loaded up all my gear and my inexperienced son. He slept most of the way there, and we arrived around daybreak. We had the best time putting on the camouflage and retrofitting the gear onto our bodies. It was like we were Navy SEALs preparing for a mission. We walked the entire property the first morning and tried to hunt slowly. It wasn't the best strategy, but I doubted my teenage hunting partner could endure an extended sit in a tree stand—at least not on his first day. So we were off like Vikings exploring a new country. The deer were pretty safe, but we had a great time.

We arrived back at my SUV around nine in the morning. We were both tired and hungry but in a great mood; this may have been the best time I'd had with my son up to that point in his life. There can be a deep connection between a father and his son in the quiet woods. The wilderness has a way of drawing men out of themselves.

At the SUV, I had planned a "man-breakfast" for us that I laid out on the hood of the SUV. I brought cereal, milk, and spoons but purposefully forgot the bowls. I placed the cereal box on its side and cut it open with my hunting knife. We poured the milk in and ate like starved warriors—right out of the box! After breakfast, I felt a pull in my spirit to say some things to my son. It honestly had not been a spiritual morning, but the significance of my feelings would not go away. I turned to my son and began to speak life into him. He was already in love with Jesus, studying God's Word, and reading books from influential godly authors. However, he was still searching for his calling and unsure of his gifting. So, I spoke using my father voice. I remember many of the personal and heartfelt messages I shared with my son. The Spirit of God did what He wants us to do—He used a father's voice to call out a son's future. My son wept, and his father cried with him. It was one of the best mornings either of us ever had.

One of the reasons we have such an identity crisis in our culture is the lack of fatherly voices, especially from spiritual fathers. Amazingly, most dads portrayed in television shows and movies these days are of questionable character and low intellect. Almost all of them are seeking to evade their fatherly responsibilities. The mothers, not the fathers, display the strongest voices. Why would we minimize dads when we need them now more than ever? The reason is both simple and sinister. The enemy knows that the best way to keep us trapped in our dysfunction is to keep fathers from being functional. The enemy of your soul is terrified by the power of the father voice.

It is interesting to note our lack of information on David's immediate family. You might read about this amazing man and think he had some historical or genealogical advantage. Nothing could be further from the truth. David faced the same lack that many of us face. David had to find "replacement relationships" to fill the gaping holes in his world that were supposed to be filled by family. But this is what our God does! Everyone is born with a family they did not choose. We treasure and love them and are a part of the imperfection. Then, we meet Jesus, and He begins to fill the gaps. He helps us find a spiritual family through His church. For some, this may be the only family you have. David wrote, *"God places the lonely in families"* (Psalm 68:6). He also wrote that God is *"Father to the fatherless"* (Psalm 68:5). God wants to fill the canyons of need in your life with the rich relationships only He can provide. This includes father voices who can speak what should have already been spoken.

FATHER GOD

Fifty-three times in the Gospels, Jesus uses the phrase *"My Father."* Twenty-three times, He uses the phrase *"Our Father."* It

GOD WANTS TO FILL THE
CANYONS OF NEED IN YOUR LIFE
WITH THE RICH RELATIONSHIPS
ONLY HE CAN PROVIDE.

makes sense that our spiritual God chose to represent Himself as Father. God decided to use the most intimate and powerful relational identity to define Himself for us. God knew that we earthly fathers would fail. God knew that some fathers would abandon or even abuse their children. God understood the generational effect that we fathers have. If your father pushed you down, he was likely pushed down by his father. Numbers 14:18 (KJV, NKJV) tells us that fathers' *"iniquity"* (the historical sin) can be passed down to the third and fourth generations. God knew we fathers would operate under this curse. God knew He would need to be a *Father* to us. He knew that only His voice would be powerful enough to teach us to be fathers.

Jesus said, *"If you then, evil as you are, know how to give good gifts [gifts that are to their advantage] to your children, how much more will your heavenly Father give the Holy Spirit to those who ask and continue to ask Him!"* (Luke 11:13 AMPC). The gift the Father wants to give us requires that we have a close relationship with the Holy Spirit. The Holy Spirit magnifies the voice of your heavenly Father. You will never truly know who God is until you experience Him as your Father. This Spirit-driven relationship is where the deepest forms of restoration are found.

I witnessed this kind of healing happen to a young man at one of the camps I spoke at years ago. Standing on the stage, I was led by the Spirit to speak to the young men about identity. Afterward, I was approached by a young man whose parents had planted within him a false narrative about his identity. I told him to pray and ask God to show him who he was. An hour later, he came to me and showed me twenty pages of journal pages that he had just written. The Father lavishly showed His son his true, God-given identity. This young man was overjoyed because God had spoken clearly to him. This is what God the Father wants to do for each of us.

David's life was a raw example of our desperate need for the Father's voice. During every powerful event in David's life, we see him communicating with God the Father first. When we see David get off track, it is always preceded by a lack of communication with God. An encounter with his heavenly Father always preceded the times David had the most powerful influence on others.

Think about this: God chose to create the world by using His voice. We see in Genesis 1 that God spoke creation into existence. Simply put, when God speaks, creation happens—true of planets and true of us. When the Father speaks to us, new worlds are created. I love that when Jesus raised Lazarus from the dead (see John 11), He used His voice to call him out of the grave. When God speaks, dead things come back to life! This is why we must hunger to know the Father's voice. There are specific messages that can be conveyed through His voice alone, resonating in ways that nothing else can. We must hear from Him first to have something to say to others.

THE FATHER BLESSING

I want to briefly stray from the story of David and show you another prolific father story from Scripture. We encounter another complicated character named Jacob almost eight hundred years before David. Like David, Jacob's story is raw and authentic. Scripture holds nothing back as it shows Jacob's failures and flourishing alike. If you are familiar with the story, you know that the most significant event in Jacob's life was the night he literally wrestled with God. (See Genesis 32:22–32.) We see Davidic principles throughout the account of Jacob's life—including his encounters with God, which set up both his relational and professional success.

While Jacob wrestled with God, he cried, *"I will not let you go unless you bless me"* (Genesis 32:26). Jacob wanted something deeper than material blessings. He wanted to know who he was. Jacob and David had to find their identities by getting close to God. In this epic encounter, God renamed Jacob. He said, *"Your name will no longer be Jacob.... From now on you will be called Israel, because you have fought with God and with men and have won"* (Genesis 32:28). God revealed Jacob's true identity to him. Jacob means "supplanter or deceiver," while Israel means "one who wrestles with God" or "Prince of God."[6]

Jacob met his heavenly Father that night, setting up one of the greatest fathering moments in the Bible. Toward the end of his life, Jacob would speak a fatherly blessing over his sons. (See Genesis 49.) Jacob had twelve sons who would eventually became the twelve tribes of Israel. In Genesis 49, Jacob called for a sacred assembly with his twelve sons, saying, *"Come and listen, you sons of Jacob; listen to Israel, your father"* (Genesis 49:2). He then spoke a prophetic fatherly blessing over each one. It is important to note that some of his "blessings" were corrective. Not even a father can bless you past your obedience. Fatherly blessing is not just about calling *up* potential but also about calling *out* rebellion.

Jacob methodically called out what he saw with his "father eyes." He called out the future in each of these twelve blessings, and the Bible record tells us that all his prophecies came true. The father voice is a prophetic voice. Jacob spoke to their

---

6. "What Does Israel Mean? Exploring This Important Biblical Name," FIRM (Fellowship of Israel Related Ministries), accessed on December 18, 2024, https://firmisrael.org/learn/what-is-the-meaning-of-the-name-israel.

character and their potential. He corrected evil, and he blessed them in his favor. Jacob was being a warrior dad, and the nation's very future depended on his generation-changing obedience.

I encourage you to study the whole blessing found in Genesis 49. For now, let's highlight what his father voice proclaimed over his son Joseph.

> *Joseph is a fruitful vine, a fruitful vine near a spring, whose branches climb over a wall.* [In other words, "Joseph, you have great potential."] *With bitterness archers attacked him; they shot at him with hostility.* [He had been wounded, and Jacob is speaking healing.] *But his bow remained steady, his strong arms stayed limber* ["You have strength, courage, and gifting."] *because of the hand of the Mighty One of Jacob, because of the Shepherd, the Rock of Israel, because of your father's God, who helps you, because of the Almighty, who blesses you with blessings of the skies above, blessings of the deep springs below, blessings of the breast and womb.* ["You are loved by God, and I see your love for God."] *Your father's blessings are greater than the blessings of the ancient mountains, than the bounty of the age-old hills. Let all these rest on the head of Joseph, on the brow of the prince among his brothers.* ["You are great in the eyes of your dad. You are special."]
>
> (Genesis 49:22–26 NIV)

Can you imagine sitting under this kind of blessing from your father? Most of us can't even fathom a moment like this because we have never experienced it. We modern fathers must relearn the lost art of blessing our children. We must bring the blessing back.

Jacob's example carries strength and a godly masculinity that can still be felt today. With our spirits, we can feel the power flowing through his vocal cords as he speaks over his precious sons. These were blessings only a father could have verbalized. His words reversed every negative label his sons had received from an insecure and cruel world. His words were restorative to the very depths of their beings. This was a moment from which they would never recover—they were forever changed.

One of the significant challenges of this book is for us to become men of blessing, spiritual dads who have spiritual sons to whom we speak life. You are not living up to your potential as a man until you call out the potential in another man. We must bring the blessing back! Why don't we start right now? I wrote a father blessing that I would like to speak over you. Why don't you read this out loud right where you are?

> As a spiritual father, today, I declare that you have great value. By the Holy Spirit, I see treasure in you—I see masculinity and courage—I see potential waiting to be fulfilled. So, I nullify every negative voice ever spoken over you, in Jesus's name. I declare that your heavenly Father's voice overrides every false word ever spoken over you! Today, you are relabeled as God's anointed one—a mighty warrior. This day, I charge you to be a father to others, even if your father was not one to you. I see a king in the making. I see calling and purpose. Pursue your Father in heaven; He will do great things through you on earth. I bless you so you can be blessing.

Do you receive that blessing? If not, then reread it aloud over yourself. Be like Jacob and read it over your literal or spiritual sons. Bring the blessing back.

Every one of us must place ourselves under positive fatherly influences. Only then can we spread the blessing by being a father to others. Fathers are essential—they are never optional. Without spiritual fathers, shepherd boys can't become kings, deceivers can't become princes, and boys can't become men. So, let's commit today to both sides of the equation: sonship and fatherhood. I am a son who needs the influence of a father. I also have a calling to be a father to a generation of searching sons. You have this same blessing and this same burden. You have a need, and you are needed.

2

ORDAINED OPPOSITION
(DAVID & GOLIATH, SAUL)

> *David asked the men standing near him, "What will be done for the man who kills this Philistine and removes this disgrace from Israel? Who is this uncircumcised Philistine that he should defy the armies of the living God?"*
> —1 Samuel 17:26 (NIV)

In certain parts of the world where forest fires are common, coniferous trees produce what are called serotinous cones. These pinecones are not just the ready-made decoration we love to put in a bowl on our mantel. They are an ingenious natural delivery system for seeds that reproduce a particular species of pine trees. Serotinous cones are unique because of the thick, strong resin covering them. This resin protects and preserves the inner seeds long after they mature. The serotinous cones open when a forest fire sweeps through, melting the resin, opening the cone, and releasing the seeds.[7]

These natural delivery systems must sit and wait for the worst thing to happen before they can perform the function God has designed them to do. Like all pinecones, serotinous cones carry within them the future of the forest. Unlike other species, these seeds have their destiny intertwined with tragedy. They long for the torridity feared by all the different trees, for only in the fire can they do what is required. They are a great illustration of the God-given potential inside each of us. Like the serotinous cones, the "seeds" of your future will require some fire. The enemy will send attacks intended to destroy us—severe heat that he thinks will consume us. But the blaze of these battles will only release what God has put in us. What Satan means for your destruction, God will redeem for your development. (See Genesis 50:20.)

Fire is often used as a metaphor for opposition. A destructive fire is an opposing force, both literally and figuratively. However, that same element of fire that can destroy can also be used to forge steel, or combust gas and run an engine. Opposition can take us out or carry us into all we are meant to have and form us into the men God created us to be. We see this early and often throughout the story of David. We see a bold rise in opposition every time God gives David an opportunity. You could even say that David's opposition was the fire needed to release and germinate the seeds of opportunity in his life. His opposition was also his God-ordained opportunity. We see this effect in his defeat

---

7. Luba Mullen, "How Trees Survive and Thrive After a Fire," *Your National Forests Magazine*, Summer/Fall 2017, National Forest Foundation, https://www.nationalforests.org/our-forests/light-and-seed-magazine/how-trees-survive-and-thrive-after-a-fire#:~:text=.

of Goliath and King Saul's nearly decade-long attack against him. This opposition, mixed with opportunity, continues with David facing haters throughout his embattled but blessed life. Want to be like David? Be careful what you wish for! When you pray for promotion, you invite resistance.

The Bible is rich with the truth of the marriage between our struggle and advancement. It is emphasized repeatedly in the lives of countless characters who faced battles before blessings. Yet, Peter and James tell us we should be "joyful" about opposition and welcome it as an opportunity for growth and maturation.

> *So be truly glad. There is wonderful joy ahead, even though you must endure many trials for a little while. These trials will show that your faith is genuine. It is being tested as fire tests and purifies gold—though your faith is far more precious than mere gold. So when your faith remains strong through many trials, it will bring you much praise and glory and honor on the day when Jesus Christ is revealed to the whole world.* (1 Peter 1:6–7)

Faith is not *faith* until it is tested. The fire of opposition transforms your elementary belief in Jesus into the golden faith He wants you to have! Your trial possesses a power of formation that can purify you and shape you into something far greater than you would ever be without it.

James is even more literal about this great truth. He says, "When troubles of any kind come your way, consider it an opportunity for great joy" (James 1:2). What? How can a trial be an opportunity of joy? This is truly a divine perspective. When most of us see a Goliath or are being chased by a relentless Saul, we become so overly aware of the opposition that we become blind to the opportunity. We certainly are not joyful about it! Our anxiety kills our vision, and we become trauma victims instead of disciples being formed by the trial.

What if we shifted our mentality and became brave again? Like a naïve, young David, we could rush the battle lines (see 1 Samuel 17:48) and meet our foe with courageous faith instead of over-developed fears. I love how *The Message* translation paraphrases James 1:2–4:

> *Consider it a sheer gift, friends, when tests and challenges come at you from all sides. You know that under pressure, your faith-life is forced into the open and shows its true colors. So don't try to get out of anything prematurely. Let it do its work so you become mature and well-developed, not deficient in any way.*

Your challenges and all the pressure you are facing are a gift if your obedience to God has triggered the rise of your adversary. "*So don't try to get out of anything prematurely*"—embrace the fight, relish it, and tap the resource of your opposition. Use it as fuel for your future. You require the fire you are facing.

What is your relationship with the Goliath in your life? Is it an association you are trying to avoid? A bond you desperately want to break? No one wants opposition; we all would love to have calm seas for the rest of our days. But our desire for ease can be more dangerous than a well-armed nine-foot-tall giant. Goliaths are emboldened by avoidance. Giants do not go away on their own; they must be forced to do so. The one David met in the Valley of Elah had mocked Israel forty days in a row. (See 1 Samuel 17:16.) God could have stopped him, but He didn't. This was God-ordained opposition.

Goliath may have struck fear into the Israelites, but not into David. The defeat of the Philistine would serve as his royal coming-out party. Goliath would pave David's way to the palace. It is a strange truth, but, actually, David needed Goliath. Why? Because it is only in the fire that we become warriors. God has ordained opponents for everyone He uses in the kingdom. David had to experience the burden of facing Goliath (and others) before he could bear the weight of the throne.

GIANT PROMOTIONS

One of the many things I love about the record of David is how God kept remembering him. In chapter 1, we see David's father and brothers forget to tell David about Samuel's search for the next king of Israel. God relentlessly refused to let David be ruled out. People may forget you, but God's promotions will still find you.

> *All these blessings shall come upon you and overtake you, because you obey the voice of the LORD your God.*
> (Deuteronomy 28:2 NKJV)

David proclaimed, *"Certainly goodness and faithfulness will follow me all the days of my life"* (Psalm 23:6 NASB). The Hebrew word *radaph* means to pursue, chase, or follow after. Are you feeling stuck, or are the desires and dreams of your heart larger than those of your current situation? You do not need to worry about how or when your promotion will come. Chase, pursue, and follow God just like David did. God's advancements and blessings will overwhelm you.

In 1 Samuel 17, the Philistines invaded the Valley of Elah, the last geographical blockade before invading Israel itself. The Israelite army prepared for a confrontation, but David's name was left off the invite list. David was completely out of position and forgotten. He was fifteen miles away in the fields outside Bethlehem, tending his father's sheep. The future king showed obedience and faithfulness in the monotony of his lowly assignment. Greatness is formed by serving.

In 1 Samuel 17:17–18, Jesse asked David to take some food to his brothers and check on them. (David could have added "food deliverer" and "low-level spy for a nosey father" to his list of responsibilities.) Israel's next king was given an assignment that would impress absolutely no one. This is the way God works. God will send a giant promotion on a typical day while you're performing an insignificant job. God's timing is perfection—it was for David and will be for you.

Goliath looked insurmountable and invincible to everyone else—except David. No matter how many times I survey the text, I cannot find evidence of even an ounce of fear in David. He spoke to or about Goliath as if the Philistine were already defeated. In contrast, all the trained, professional soldiers were so terrified that they would flee in great terror whenever Goliath appeared. (See 1 Samuel 17:24.) David did not see Goliath as a threat; he saw Goliath as a giant opportunity.

David heard the giant's *"usual defiance"* (verse 23 NIV), and instead of his reacting in fear, David asked, *"What will be done for the man who kills this Philistine and removes this disgrace from Israel?"* (1 Samuel 17:26 NIV). What a response from a seventeen-year-old who had never been trained as a soldier! When I first read it, I thought it might look like arrogance or ignorance. It could be simple self-promotion—after all, David was human, and I am sure he wanted to get out of those fields where his sheep grazed. However, the more I look at the text and ask the

Holy Spirit to show me what is happening, the more I see the purity of David's response.

The very next sentence out of David's mouth is about glorifying God, not himself. *"Who is this uncircumcised Philistine that he should defy the armies of the living God?"* (1 Samuel 17:26 NIV). David was offended on behalf of God, not himself. David wanted God's name to be protected, not his own name to be promoted. He revealed his holy motive for victory in verse 46 when he said, *"The whole world will know that there is a God in Israel. All those gathered here will know that it is not by sword or spear that the LORD saves; for the battle is the LORD's, and he will give all of you into our hands"* (1 Samuel 17:46–47 NIV). David wanted the entire world to know how great his God was. David wanted to make God famous, not himself.

How could David see opportunity when everyone else saw only opposition? There are two significant reasons for this: *motive* and *mindset*. If you pursue promotion with the wrong motive, even the right mindset will not help you. Your self-glorifying heart will sabotage even a God-given opportunity. On the other hand, if your motive is pure but your mindset is one of fear and resignation, you will be defeated before you even face your opposition.

David had spent thousands of lonely hours as a shepherd. Instead of wasting that time, he used it to get to know God's heart. If you get to know God's heart, He will purify yours. He also learned about God's power as he fought the beasts who tried to attack his sheep. It was in this training ground that David developed a divine perspective. Goliath looked small when he stood before David because David's God was so big. This is the power of a pure heart and a righteous mind.

WHEN I ENCOUNTER THOSE
WHO OPPOSE ME, I DO NOT WANT
TO FORGET THAT GOD IS FOR
ME. I WANT TO INSTINCTIVELY
KNOW THAT OPPOSITION
IS AN OPPORTUNITY FOR
GROWTH AND EVEN A PATHWAY
TO BLESSING.

There have been volumes of books and millions of sermons written on David. However, it is essential to note that David's life is not a methodology to master but a model from which to learn. David's courageous encounter with Goliath seems to come naturally. This is not a formula David is trying to follow. He had not read a book on the *Three Easy Steps to Defeat the Giants of Your Life*. No, David became what he was practicing. He spent time with God. His bravery flowed from his established identity, and his confidence reflected his spiritual authenticity.

I do not want to be David; rather, I want to possess his beautiful character traits. When I encounter those who oppose me, I do not want to forget that God is for me. I want to instinctively know that opposition is an opportunity for growth and even a pathway to blessing. I want faith to be so normal that I regularly experience the supernatural. I want to face my giants the way David faced his. The only way a "Goliath" can kill a "David" is if he can somehow make him forget who he is. Stop forgetting who you are! You are God's man, and the opposition you face will only serve to position you for what God has for you. Goliaths may seem big, but your God is infinitely bigger.

PUSHING PAST DECEITFUL DISTRACTIONS

Following the text's chronological order, you will see that David faced a major distraction immediately after he inquired about Goliath. It was a deceit-filled attack from someone who had access. This is a pattern you see emerge anytime you go after what God has for you. The enemy always sends distractions when we are about to embrace our destinies. In this case, it is an inside job. David's older brother Eliab stepped in his way. He disapproved of what David was doing. Eliab had power at this moment because younger brothers always want their older brothers' approval. Just as Jesse had done, Eliab disdained and disrespected David.

> *When Eliab, David's oldest brother, heard him speaking with the men, he burned with anger at him and asked, "Why have you come down here? And with whom did you leave those few sheep in the wilderness? I know how conceited you are and how wicked your heart is; you came down only to watch the battle."* (1 Samuel 17:28 NIV)

There is much to unpack here. Eliab uses his words like an evil swordsman as he attempts to cut David down to size. He questions his heart and attempts to push him back into the sheep fields.

Eliab's offense was partially based on his cowardice. He was one of the terrified soldiers who was unwilling to fight Goliath. David was deeply hurt, but he refused to take the bait. *"David turned away from Eliab"* (1 Samuel 17:30 AMP). Why engage an agitator when your assignment awaits you in the valley? The enemy loves it when we fight our Eliabs. He knows if he can keep you off mission, then the giants of your life will remain undefeated. Winston Churchill once said, "You will never reach your destination if you stop and throw stones at every dog that barks." This is the warning found in Eliab for all of us! You cannot engage your distraction and defeat your opposition simultaneously. Opportunities are lost when we engage in lesser things.

DEFYING RAGGED RESUMES

> *What David said was overheard and reported to Saul, and Saul sent for him.* (1 Samuel 17:31 NIV)

I am sure King Saul saw what everyone else did. David did not look like a warrior, and Saul did not have the eyes of a prophet. David was young, inexperienced, and lacking in training. Despite all this, David decided to give his best interview speech when he approached Saul. He spoke of caring for his father's sheep and of having killed a lion and a bear when they came looking for a free meal. He compared the impending defeat of the Philistine army to his minor victorious battles and assured Saul that he would kill the giant. (See 1 Samuel 17:34–37.)

I find this part of the story quite humorous. Confronting Goliath was the most important job in Israel. David was making a case based on his only accomplishments. His resume was thin, but he put it on thick stock paper and read it with gusto before King Saul. David must have sounded like a former shift manager of a fast-food restaurant applying to be the CEO of a Fortune 500 company. Saul had to have known that David was not qualified. Maybe he was blinded by his desperation. The Israelites had endured forty days of taunts and threats without anyone in their camp stepping up to the challenge. Could it have been David's passionate charisma and anointing that made Saul agree? To everyone's surprise, the king said, "*Go, and the* L<small>ORD</small> *be with you*" (1 Samuel 17:37 NIV). Saul had no idea he was hiring his future replacement. Only God could have predicted what would happen next.

The following verses capture another unintentionally funny scene:

> *Then Saul dressed David in his own tunic. He put a coat of armor on him and a bronze helmet on his head. David fastened on his sword over the tunic and tried walking around,*

> because he was not used to them. "I cannot go in these," he said to Saul, "because I am not used to them." So he took them off. (1 Samuel 17:38–39 NIV)

Can you envision David swimming in armor that was too large for him? I love the phrase *"I am not used to them."* David was not far removed from his long, lonely days as a shepherd. He had never worn traditional armor and maybe had never even wielded a sword. He certainly had never faced a trained soldier like Goliath. So, he wanted what he was *"used to."* It is your history that prepares you for your future. It is the weapons you develop in private (while no one is watching) that God will one day use in public (while everyone is watching). The sheep field had prepared David for the battlefield.

David chose the weapons of a shepherd: a staff, a sling, and five smooth stones. Shepherds were known to carry a sling for throwing stones because stones were a formidable weapon and did not take up much room. Research indicates that a sling like that of David could sling a rock at over 60 miles per hour for approximately 656 feet. Armies of that day would even have divisions of slingers due to their quickness, efficiency, and lethal capabilities. I believe that David was very skilled with this weapon. As a shepherd, what else did you have to do during a long afternoon watching sheep? I bet David had knocked the bark off every tree surrounding those fields. He was confident in the skills he had honed while shepherding. He had experienced the power of God as he was faithful in defending his sheep. His seemingly insignificant moments of obedience set him up for a big victory. The principle is powerful: If you fail to win the small battles of your life, you will never defeat the giants. However, if you are faithful to defeat your lions and bears, your Goliaths don't stand a chance.

Do you know the rest of the story? David and Goliath traded barbs of spiritual trash talk (see 1 Samuel 17:42–47), but in the end, we know that David stood before Saul with Goliath's head. The Bible says he carried the head back to Jerusalem. (See 1 Samuel 17:54.) No one dared to call him a shepherd boy after his victory. Everyone saw what God already knew—David was a warrior destined to be king. I love the latter part of the verse that says that *"he put the Philistine's weapons in his own tent"* (1 Samuel 17:54 NIV). He eventually lost track of it, but in 1 Samuel 21, David was reunited with Goliath's sword. When he found it, David proclaimed, *"There is no other sword like it"* (1 Samuel 21:9 NCV). The weapon of an evil-hearted giant became the sword of a pure-hearted warrior. When you kill a "Goliath" yourself, my advice is: keep the sword. There is sure to be another giant. Obedience invites opposition. You can't have one without the other.

CONQUERING EXTENDED ENEMIES

> *Saul became even more afraid of him, and he remained David's enemy for the rest of his life.* (1 Samuel 18:29)

The story of Goliath's defeat is a fun one to preach and a joy to write about. It is so powerful because it is so uncomplicated. The giant stood tall but fell hard. He may have been frightening, but his reign of terror didn't last long. David defeats the giant. In fact, it is on the first day David meets Goliath that he kills him. The conflict is resolved as fast as it arises—Goliath rose and fell in fifty-eight verses, even with a commercial break about Eliab in the middle of the story.

If only all relational challenges were resolved this cleanly. But that is not the case for us, and it certainly was not for David.

IF YOU FAIL TO WIN THE SMALL BATTLES OF YOUR LIFE, YOU WILL NEVER DEFEAT THE GIANTS. HOWEVER, IF YOU ARE FAITHFUL TO DEFEAT YOUR LIONS AND BEARS, YOUR GOLIATHS DON'T STAND A CHANCE.

His next ordained opposition would be in his life for a decade, and subsidiary conflicts stemming from it would last much longer. This long, stubborn kind of opposition was not so much about his promotion as it was the development of his character. We need both. David's conflict with King Saul would be much more formidable than his skirmish with Goliath. Saul was the gift David didn't ask for. He was the resistance who refused to relent.

David found himself in a relationship with Saul through no fault of his own. He didn't ask to be called out of a field and to be tapped as the next king of Israel. It was David's faithfulness that led him to the throne of King Saul. It was his obedience to his God-given calling that put David in the path of Saul's wrath. David did not ask to have spears thrown at him or to be hunted for years on end. He certainly did not deserve the slander and false accusations.

The same man who slayed a giant would write, *"I am forgotten like a dead man, and out of mind; like a broken vessel am I"* (Psalm 31:12 AMPC). Scholars believe that David wrote this psalm while he was being hunted by King Saul. God was not explaining Himself to David as he ran for his life. He must have been thinking, "How did all this happen? How did I get myself and my family into this mess?" In his own words, David said he was *"broken."* This does not mean he was broken in will or spirit. It means David was being broken down and rebuilt by God. He was being formed into the man God needed him to be. God used a madman to form a masterpiece. God used Saul to form the greatest king the world has ever seen.

David accidentally (but providentially) enrolled in an unknown university that has no buildings and gives out no diplomas—a school where God Himself is the President. The only professors are relationships with people who cause unwanted difficulty and pain. The students are all chosen by God to do something great in His kingdom. The name of this hidden institution is the "University of Brokenness." Anyone who wants to maximize their divine potential must walk its halls and take its tests.[8]

The words of the last paragraph are paraphrased from a classic work by Gene Edwards called *A Tale of Three Kings*. I learned this concept thirty-five years ago in my first ministry assignment out of Bible college. God led me to a church without telling me that the leader was a lot like Saul. This pastor's favorite hurtful phrase was, "Welcome to the ministry." He used it as a covering for all the abuse he piled on me. I served under him for a little over a year and questioned why I had ever gone into ministry. I was broken, and it felt like there was no strategy for coping with what I was going through. My decision to obey God had positioned me to experience pain.

I have seen this pattern emerge as I've talked with many friends over the years. Many great men of God have the same story about some of their early God-given assignments. A. W. Tozer said, "It is doubtful whether God can bless a man greatly until he has hurt him deeply." Truths like this can only be learned in the school of brokenness.

In the middle of that challenging year, I read *A Tale of Three Kings*. It's a book I believe every man should read. Edwards writes in allegorical style about King Saul, King David, and David's son Absalom. This book found me when I needed to understand why God would ever call anyone to serve under

---

8. Gene Edwards, *A Tale of Three Kings: A Study in Brokenness* (Carol Stream, IL: Tyndale House, 1992), 22.

a Saul-like leader. In the fifth chapter of this masterpiece, Edwards writes:

> God has a university. It's a small school. Few enroll; even fewer graduate. Very, very few indeed. God has this school because he does not have broken men and women. He has people who claim to have God's authority...and don't—people who claim to be broken...and aren't. And people who do have God's authority but are mad *and* unbroken. And he has, regretfully, a great mixture of everything in between. All of these he has in abundance, but broken men and women, hardly at all.[9]

He writes, "David was once a student in this school, and Saul was God's chosen way to crush David."[10] According to Edwards (and the Bible), everyone needs a God-ordained relationship with someone like Saul.

If you are new to this kind of biblical narrative or experience, you might ask, "How could God ever use a person like King Saul?" You might even ask, "How could God love me and ordain me to go through the kind of frustration and pain David went through?" These questions are good if they lead you to a place of godly brokenness. God loves it when we ask, but He will not always answer. Understanding is overrated. If you understood everything, you would never grow in your faith. David's story can guide you out of your wilderness because you have an informed view of his experience. We know how the story ends. David had to trust without knowing the outcome.

My favorite moment of David's extended encounters with Saul happened in a cave near the Crags of the Wild Goats. We

---
9. Edwards, *Tale of Three Kings*, 22.
10. Edwards, *Tale of Three Kings*, 22.

don't name places as good as they did in the Bible; what a name! In 1 Samuel 24, we find David and his men on the run from this now-madman King Saul. The Bible says that while David and his men were hiding in the cave, Saul came in to *"relieve himself"* (1 Samuel 24:3). You can't make this stuff up. While Saul was in a vulnerable position, David's men begin whispering, *"Now's your opportunity!...Today the L*ORD *is telling you, 'I will certainly put your enemy into your power, to do with as you wish'"* (1 Samuel 24:4). Instead David only crawled forward and cut off a piece of Saul's robe so he could later show him he had had the chance to kill him but refrained. Later, David even felt bad about doing that! Only brokenness can make you cut a robe when your flesh wants to slit a throat.

Despite King Saul's deceitful, murderous behavior, David focused on obeying the Lord. David said, *"The L*ORD *forbid that I should do this thing to my master, the L*ORD*'s anointed, to stretch out my hand against him, seeing he is the anointed of the L*ORD*"* (1 Samuel 24:6 NKJV). This is brokenness at its best, doing its work in a man who refuses to promote himself. David knew his story was God's story, and he would not take the pen out of God's hands. David would not murder his way to the throne.

Think about it for a minute: one day, David would have to explain how he had become king. Decades later, one of his grandkids would crawl onto his lap and ask about the details. Killing the former king while he was going to the bathroom would not be an honorable story! Self-promotion is never a bestseller because it is so common. But the man who trusts God and refuses to elevate himself, even when he has the power to do so, is always an epic tale. I want the narrative of my life to be that I trusted Him and honored Him no matter how many spears

Saul threw my way. The only stories that bring Him glory are the ones He writes for us, not the ones we write for ourselves.

DIVINE LIMITS

A few years ago, we were gifted a precious Yorkie puppy. We raised her for a year or so before we decided to give her to some dear friends because my ever-growing travel schedule made it too difficult for us to take care of her. We named her Maizy, and we still love it when she comes for a visit. When little Maizy first arrived at our home, she weighed only about four pounds. At the time, a large dog was living next door to us. The neighbors had installed an invisible fence around their property, and their dog wore a shock collar. I am not a fan of the system, but it was very effective. The dog never crossed his property line.

One evening, I let Maizy out our back door. Seeing our large, furry neighbor, she took off like a rocket toward him, and he returned the favor. I thought for sure she was a goner. She was running at him like she was a trained Belgian Malinois, and I was the Navy SEAL who had given her a kill order. Just as Maizy arrived face-to-face with the other dog, he slid to a dead stop. He had reached the edge of his range and did not want to be shocked. Maizy barked at the edge of our property line with all the anger her four-pound body could muster. She kept looking back at me as if to say, "Are you seeing this? I could totally take him; let me kill him, Dad." It was one of the funniest things I have ever witnessed. She could not be contained for weeks after that.

Sometimes, it may seem as if God is allowing our opposition to be unlimited. It might look like the Goliaths and Sauls can come at us at will. Yet nothing could be further from the truth. A close reading of David's life reveals that divine precision often resembles chaos. God knew whom David needed and how long he needed them. This is true for you and me, as well. He will only let your opposition have so much access. Your enemies may encroach on you and even get to land some punches, but they cannot cancel your divine purpose. They cannot define who you are. Only God has authority over your identity, and only He can define your calling. Your opposition may seem prolonged and your deliverance delayed, but, like David, you will arrive at your place of purpose at the divinely appointed time.

David wrote, "*You are my hiding place; You shall preserve me from trouble; You shall surround me with songs of deliverance*" (Psalm 32:7 NKJV). Would David have known where to hide if he did not have someone chasing him? Would he have known deliverance if he had never been in danger? Would he have written such memorable songs about his God if he had not experienced the silence of the wilderness?

We learn from David that God uses friends and foes to form us. The wondrous and weighty plans of God always include roses and thorns. Kingdom relationships are a package deal. If we try to avoid painful relationships, we will forfeit their purpose, which is hidden in God's plan. Goliaths will propel you toward the palace, and Sauls will prepare you for the throne. There is opportunity in opposition.

3

COVENANT FRIENDSHIP (DAVID & JONATHAN)

Then Jonathan made a covenant with David because he loved him as himself.
—1 Samuel 18:3 (AMP)

I grew up across the street from my best friend. His name is Keith, and we have been inseparable since we were kids. I cannot remember a season when he was not part of my life. Unlike myself, Keith grew up in church. I knew about this part of his life, but we never discussed it. Then, at sixteen, Keith's walk with Jesus went to another level. This led to a burden for my salvation. I was lost; I needed Jesus. Keith invited me to church on a Monday night. His church was having a special set of meetings targeting unbelievers. That courageous invitation changed everything for me.

Keith didn't know that I had been trying to read the Bible for several weeks. I had a desire for change, and I was so depressed that I was suicidal. He also did not know I had tickets to a Van Halen concert that Monday night. What can I say? It was the '80s—rock on! I had plans to get drunk that night and do anything else I could to have fun and feel free. To Keith's surprise—and to my own—I gave up my concert tickets and went to church. I was desperate for something different, and I trusted my friend.

Keith's church was charismatic and filled with life. The speaker was dynamic, and he shared the gospel of Jesus in a clear, dynamic way. I wanted to change so badly that I ignored any parts of the service I couldn't understand. I felt the joy that was there, and I wanted what they had. In the end, they invited people to come down front and "accept Jesus." I felt compelled, but I did not respond. Then they announced there would be another service the next night (Keith had not told me they were having two weeks of services). I asked if I could come back, and he was thrilled. That Tuesday night in 1984, I knelt at the altar of that church and gave my life to Jesus. He forgave my sins and filled me with joy and peace that are still in me today. You do not know how heavy sin is until it is gone! I attended that church for the next two years, and then I headed off to Bible college to prepare for what would become over thirty years of ministry. Thank God for a friend who cared enough to invite me into his world. Without him, this very book would have never been written.

I really owe everything I have to the person who introduced me to Jesus. Without my salvation, I would not be alive, let alone have the family, friends, or life I enjoy. I certainly would not be an author, pastor, or missionary. I would not have traveled the world and helped many others come to Jesus. I would not be forgiven, and I would not have the peace I walk in every day. Keith's friendship led me to the most significant relationship a person can ever have: a relationship with Jesus. Maybe you don't have a friend like I did. Perhaps someone gave you this book because you are missing something; you have a void in you that cannot seem to be filled. You need Jesus. Why not pray this simple prayer right now? Pray it out loud right where you are:

> Dear Jesus, I believe You died on the cross and rose from the dead. I believe You are real. Please save me from my sin and from myself. Wash away my guilt and make me a new person. Lead me. Give me the life I was meant to live.

If you authentically prayed that simple prayer, God heard you, and you are saved! Welcome to the brotherhood! Welcome to the family of God!

I often tell my friend Keith that whoever I lead to Christ does not go to my "account" in heaven. All the impact of my life and ministry exists only because Keith was obedient to invite me to a place where I could meet Jesus. I also let my friend know that he is "stuck" with me—he has a friend for life, whether he likes it or not. He can try to run, but I will chase him. Keith would tell you that I have been faithful to that promise. It has led to one of the richest relationships I have ever had. Keith is not as expressive as I am, but I have received several texts and verbal messages from him indicating the same level of commitment to our friendship. Our friendship is a covenant friendship based not only on our deep past but also on our relationships with Jesus. Every person needs a friendship like that—especially men.

MIRACLE CONNECTIONS

Right up front, I want to deal with our Western mindset toward the close friendship we will study in this chapter. I have traveled extensively, and in many cultures, I see an affectionate level of friendship that is different from what Americans experience. In other parts of the world, close friends will hold hands while walking down the street and express themselves in other ways through words and physical touch. We must approach the Scriptures with a recognition of biblical culture and realize that our culture has skewed our view of such things. David and Jonathan were both warriors in the strongest sense of the word. Their masculinity should never be questioned because of their affection for each other. Some have approached their relationship with an agenda to back up a personal or societal narrative. They place things in this story that simply are not there. This covenant friendship we will study is a pure miracle from God.

Although there is some debate, there seems to be very little gap in Scripture between David's surprising friendship with Jonathan and his public victory over Goliath. The Bible tells us that David met with Saul while still holding the head of Goliath in his hand (see 1 Samuel 17:57), and they immediately discussed David's background with Jonathan (Saul's son) listening in. *"When David had finished speaking to Saul, the soul of Jonathan was bonded to the soul of David, and Jonathan loved him as himself"* (1 Samuel 18:1 AMP). The blood dripping from the severed head of Goliath had not even coagulated yet, and David already had a miracle connection—a friendship he desperately needed.

Jonathan was an unexpected ally because he was the son of King Saul. He was a prince and the assumed future king of Israel. Yet, the very person who should've been threatened by David instead had a God-given affection—a holy admiration—for David. The text says, *"Jonathan made a covenant with David because he loved him as himself"* (1 Samuel 18:3 AMP). This covenant happened quickly. Jonathan encountered someone with the same spirit he had, and he was drawn to him. Even more, Jonathan loved God like David did, and he was a warrior. Their similarities of passion fueled their friendship at a record pace. Have you ever met someone you just had to be friends with? This is the same, with a hefty dose of God's providence. Jonathan has met his best friend.

We modern men are not used to the friendship language used in Scripture. Consider this phrase: *"Jonathan became one in spirit with David, and he loved him as himself"* (1 Samuel 18:1 NIV). Jonathan swore that he would do anything to protect David from his father, King Saul. (See 1 Samuel 20:4.) David spoke about loyalty and called Jonathan his *"sworn friend."* (See 1 Samuel 20:8). Later in that same chapter, there is talk about oaths and even more covenants. In the last verse of this chapter, Jonathan said to David, *"The LORD is the witness of a bond between us and our children forever"* (1 Samuel 20:42). Who talks like this? We sure don't anymore. Maybe we should. Maybe we need to bring back the honor of covenants so we might experience the blessing of true friendship. We have either forgotten how to have covenants between us or we have never seen them modeled. We will need God to work with us if we are going to change that.

When Jonathan witnessed David's unbelievable faith and courage, his soul *"was knit with the soul of David"* (1 Samuel 18:1

KJV). Only the Holy Spirit works at the soul level like that. This is not simple human admiration. This is a weaving together of purposes. It is like a godly partnership between two civilizations—a friendship that will change nations. David did not know it at the moment, but his friendship with Jonathan would save his life several times. Jonathan had no idea that his friendship with David would bless him generationally, even after his death.

True, God-given covenant friendships are bigger than the sum of their parts. This relationship would outlive and outpace David and Jonathan so much that we are still impacted by it today. There is a multiplication effect when two callings come together for a kingdom purpose. This is what Jonathan's friendship did for David. Alone, he was powerful, but only with the help of Jonathan could David navigate the treacherous waters that surrounded his kingly calling. David needed a miracle right away, and God gave one in the implausible form of Prince Jonathan. We all need a relational miracle like this.

EQUALITY ESTABLISHED

The covenant between David and Jonathan was not a signed contract with documented terms and conditions. Relationships like theirs are vast in scope and contain too many hidden treasures; a written scroll couldn't contain them. Their covenant was made of words, but actions sealed it. The bravery of their brotherhood backed it up. The first act of courage between David and Jonathan is packed with symbolic meaning. *"Jonathan sealed the pact by taking off his robe and giving it to David, together with his tunic, sword, bow, and belt"* (1 Samuel 18:4). The obvious truth is these two men were extremely far apart from a social and economic standpoint. This fact would be a very big deal in their Eastern culture. Yet Jonathan did not wait to equalize the scales. He literally and symbolically tipped the scales by giving David his royal robe and weapons. This would have spoken volumes, not only to David but to everyone in Israel.

Jonathan could have easily thought, "I want to be friends with this guy, but he had better not forget that I am the prince." Even if not verbalized, this gap in status had to have been on David's mind. Worse yet, those around the prince would surely have highlighted the superiority of Jonathan's position.

Jonathan was living out Philippians 2:3: *"Don't be selfish; don't try to impress others. Be humble, thinking of others as better than yourselves."* In one sweeping action, he let David and the world know that they were equals. For an authentic friendship to live, superiority must die. We have all experienced relationships where this was not the case. One gives, and the other takes. One is a servant, and the other is a user. Jonathan would have none of that—superiority poisons covenants. So, Jonathan created a level playing field that became the launching pad for one of the most incredible friendships the world ever witnessed.

Mark Twain once wrote, "Keep away from people who try to belittle your ambitions. Small people always do that, but the really great make you feel that you, too, can become great."[11] Great people do not just walk around in royal clothing in front of you. The truly great give you a robe you can wear because they see royalty in you. We all need people who will selflessly "dress" us and "arm" us for the battles they know we will face. If you are struggling to think of any covenant friendships in your life or even the possibility of who they might be, let me give you some direction: enter a season of personal evaluation. Ask your-

---

11. Gay Zenola MacLaren, *Morally We Roll Along*, Section: I Meet Mark Twain (Boston, MA: Little, Brown and Company, 1938), 66.

FOR AN AUTHENTIC FRIENDSHIP
TO LIVE, SUPERIORITY MUST DIE.

self: am I alienating the people around me with intentional or unintentional superiority in my words and actions? If Jonathan had not quickly removed this possibility, the poisonous seeds of jealousy and insecurity could have quickly taken root.

If we rush here, we will miss a massive truth. Jonathan's strategic gift-giving deserves some deeper application. It may not be culturally significant for us to give out robes and swords anymore, but our imaginations can still find a way to excel at giving gifts. It's a simple but powerful practice. I have gifted all kinds of things to the men I share my life with—everything from books and Bibles to hats, knives, and fishing rods. Many of our fathers or grandfathers sought to give us gifts that they believed would speak to our masculinity, promote generational bonds, and hold personal significance. Gifts like your first firearm, hunting equipment, a musical instrument, an old car as a restoration project, or any other gift of priceless importance will stoke the fire of togetherness between men. I like giving something that closely bonds us and calls out the direction of God in the person's life. I often give away things that are imprinted with the logo of our missions organization because every man is called to help someone else. It's a bit literal, but I have also given away many compasses because God has adventures for every man to navigate. These may not be the trappings of a prince, but they speak volumes to a hungry soul in need of affirmation.

RADICAL RISK

The drama and danger of this story intensify quickly. David was in mortal danger and needed the help of his covenant friend. First Samuel 20:1 says, *"David now fled from Naioth in Ramah and found Jonathan."* The Message paraphrases David's danger by saying, *"David got out of Naioth in Ramah alive and went to*

Jonathan." In the following verses, we see David breaking the news to Jonathan about his father's murderous ways. Jonathan could not believe that his father would harm an innocent man like David. They made a plan for Jonathan to assess his father's intentions and warn David. Jonathan decided to become a spy on David's behalf, which ended up nearly costing him his life. *"Saul boiled with rage at Jonathan: 'You stupid son of a whore!' he swore at him. 'Do you think I don't know that you want him to be king in your place, shaming yourself and your mother?'"* (1 Samuel 20:30). A few verses later, *"Saul hurled his spear at Jonathan, intending to kill him"* (1 Samuel 20:33). Jonathan now understood his father's evil intentions, and the next day he warned David. They wept together and said goodbye to one another. (See 1 Samuel 20:41.) Jonathan would continue to protect David at great personal risk to himself.

One of the biggest responsibilities of a covenant friendship is protecting one another. This mandate extends to all our relationships. We should protect those weaker than us—those who cannot protect themselves. This is such a value in my life that I have developed a righteous disdain for bullies. A holy conflict rises within me whenever I see a weaker party being hurt by those with greater power. I think this is part of being a man. We even see righteous anger come out of Jesus during His ministry. (See, for example, Matthew 21:12–13.) This happened most often when there was abuse of a weaker person by the religious crowd. Protective, godly anger should be a part of any man's journey toward healthy spirituality. Men should never use these powerful emotions in an unrighteous way.

I think the first time I felt protective anger toward another person was in grade school, maybe around the fourth grade. A bully had been picking on a friend of mine, and one day after school I witnessed the bully beating up my friend, who ran away crying before I could intervene. I went home upset at what I had seen and could not shake the feeling that I had to react. My response was not the best, but it came from a good place. I was not a Christian at this time in my life, and I was immature. I remember going to the bully's house and confronting him on his porch. He showed no remorse as he stood behind a screen door, hurling profanities at me and verbally abusing my friend. He kept pressing his rather large nose against the screen door. It looked like a solid target to me, so I balled up my fist and punched the bully in the nose. He ran away crying, and I ran away because I was afraid of the consequences. I did get in a lot of trouble and had to apologize. But my friend was never picked on by the bully again.

Real friendship is not about immature confrontations on behalf of your buddies. It is about taking God-ordained risks for one another. Jonathan could see the plan of God for David as clear as day. From the first time he saw David, he realized the anointing to be king was upon David and not himself. His affection for David was not just driven by his spirit being moved; it was also incredibly wise. Jonathan could either get behind the plans of God for the throne of Israel or stand opposed to them. He could see the futile path of his father, and he wanted nothing to do with that level of self-preservation. So, the prince chose risk over safety. He would protect his friend even if it meant that the spears being thrown at David would also be thrown at him. Thank God Saul was not a very good throw.

The next time we see a risky interaction between David and Jonathan is years later while David is on the run, roaming in the wilderness with his band of warriors. *"Jonathan went to find David and encouraged him to stay strong in his faith in God. 'Don't* be afraid,' Jonathan reassured him" (1 Samuel 23:16–17). Verse 18 says, "The two of them renewed their solemn pact before the LORD." This entire moment was filled with danger for Jonathan on multiple levels. King Saul would've killed him if he found out, or David's men could've harmed or captured him as a bargaining piece against Saul. Even the travel was treacherous, as the Philistines were a constant threat. Jonathan accepted those risks because he needed to encourage his friend. Risk is right when it comes to kingdom relationships. Authentically loving a person can certainly put you in peril. I think Jonathan knew that when he made his covenant with David.

DIVINE INSIGHT

A great way to know you are supposed to be in "covenant" with someone is when you have God-given insight about them. Covenant friendships are one of the methods God uses to confirm callings and reveal buried gifting. In both the biblical narrative and my personal experience, when God calls a person, He sends several trusted voices to confirm that calling. Often, the first among these voices will be those of your intimate friends. This alone is a massive reason to pursue godly friendships. I want to have people in my life who can see my potential and help me find my path. We see clearly that when Jonathan was impressed by David, he was given "impressions" about David. These spiritual insights were so powerful that the only way they could have been shared was under the protective covering of a covenant. If you are going to accomplish your purpose, you will need people like Jonathan who can see and say what you can only sense. You will need some true, covenant friends.

Jonathan was the first person to confirm David's calling after Samuel anointed him. Think about that for a minute. I can imagine David doubting his calling, especially as he was being attacked by King Saul. He may have thought, "Sure, the old prophet could see my potential, but no one else can." We human beings usually need multiple voices of confirmation when it comes to our divine callings. Jonathan was David's second voice. *"'Don't be afraid,' Jonathan reassured him. 'My father will never find you! You are going to be the king of Israel, and I will be next to you, as my father, Saul, is well aware'"* (1 Samuel 23:17). David was running for his life, and the prince of Israel made a special trip to tell him, "You are not going to die; you will be the next king." He even double confirmed it by saying, "Even my father (the man trying to kill you) knows this to be true." Note the sacrificial humility: Jonathan proclaimed that he would be *"next to"* David. He relinquished his right to the throne on behalf of his friend. This one act by itself is astounding.

I have three people in my life whom I call pastors. I serve as a teaching pastor in three amazing churches, and I am in close partnership with each of these pastors. A covenant-style friendship is a part of my multifaceted relationship with each of these amazing men. Strangely enough, I am older than all of them, even though, in each case, they are in spiritual authority over me. All three of my pastors have shared with me divine insight they have about my gifts, my calling, and the future God has for me. In turn, I have been given deep spiritual insight about each of them, and I have often shared it with them. Our covenants with each other are a constant source of encouragement and confirmation. You might have a covenant friendship in the making if you have people in your life who keep seeing who God says you are, and you keep seeing who God says they are. Insight is a covenant indicator.

One of my pastors, Pastor Jesse, illustrated to me the power of covenant-level insight. We took a trip to Burundi, which at the time was the poorest country in the world. We had a large team there executing meaningful missions projects. In one of our final team meetings, I was sitting on the stage, talking to the team, and, for some reason, there was an empty chair next to mine. Pastor Jesse later told me that while I was talking, he could see a glow around me. He said, "God showed me how gifted and anointed you are to do the work you are called to do—the very work you were talking about on that stage." He went on to mention the grace with which I was speaking to the team and the way I had conducted myself in the difficult moments of that trip. He spoke about my vision and passion for missions. Then he mentioned the empty chair. He said, "God showed me the value of sitting next to you in this work." He spoke of the power of our "togetherness" and how much God was blessing our relationship. His words spoke into my future in a way that was so rare and so powerful that I still have not recovered from their impact. This is what covenant friends do. They see, and they say. They speak because God has given them an informed voice. This is one of many things Jonathan did for his friend David.

DEEP GRIEF

In 1 Samuel 20, in fields outside of the palace in Jerusalem, David and Jonathan received a dark revelation from God. It was as if God turned to the last chapter of the story and showed them the unending tragedy of Saul's selfish anger. This moment would mark the last time David and Jonathan would enjoy personal fellowship with each other. God revealed to them that people were going to be hurt, and their story was going to be filled with terrible turmoil. Standing in that field, the prince and the future king wept together. *"David bowed three times to Jonathan with his face to the ground. Both of them were in tears as they embraced each other and said good-bye, especially David"* (1 Samuel 20:41). The Amplified Bible, Classic Edition says that they *"wept with one another until David got control of himself."* This moment was a culmination of the abuse and attempted murder of these men at the hands of King Saul. Jonathan and *"especially David"* were in the worst moments of their lives, so they wept together. This is not the opposite of manly strength—it is the display of it. Two of the greatest warriors ever were overwhelmed by a flood of emotions so intense that the translators struggled with the words to help us understand it.

Covenant friendships should be with the people you celebrate with the most. My best friends are the people I have had the most fun with. Shared interests are a common occurrence when it comes to close friendships. The playgrounds of life are part of where deep connections are made. But it is only when the fire rages around you that you see the actual value of a loyal friend. Weeping is deeper than laughter. Covenant friendships are a place where the burdens of life are shared.

I meet men all over the country who have no one they can be vulnerable with. Worse yet, they have no one they are involved with at a deep enough level to be able to face conflict together. The two men in our text were in the fire together; the fight was infinitely bigger than them, but they did not have to face it alone. Whom would you call first, second, or third when tragedy strikes? The answers to those questions reveal the cluster of close friends you should stand united with in covenant.

I want to take a moment to offer some suggestions on how to navigate difficult times. As a society, we have not been

COVENANT FRIENDSHIPS ARE A PLACE WHERE THE BURDENS OF LIFE ARE SHARED.

very effective at this. Many men either avoid processing their emotions altogether and bury their feelings or they engage in unhealthy processing with the wrong people.

The three worst ways to process emotions are:

- Public: Not everyone should be invited into your struggle.
- Personal: You need wisdom beyond yourself.
- Purging: Only God can fully understand what you are feeling. Many words rarely lead to much wisdom.

The three best ways to process emotions are:

- Prayer: The Holy Spirit knows what you are going through.
- Private: Have a small circle of covenant people you allow into your struggle.
- Professional: Sometimes, you need trained voices to help you navigate complex situations.

It's challenging to develop healthy friendships when communication is unhealthy. Respect the boundaries of others and access your friendships with Spirit-led limitations that keep you from depleting others. As we read the story of David (the most relational person in the Bible), we do not see him being overbearing or disrespectful to the boundaries or time of Jonathan. This, too, is a part of the covenant.

SUMMARY WISDOM

If you are like me, as you study the connection between David and Jonathan, you cannot help but desire friendships like theirs. Maybe you feel as if nothing like that ever happens to you. First, I want to tell you that God has better relationships for your future than you have experienced in your past. The fact that you are reading this book means you are committed to a better relational posture that will attract better relational possibilities. Second, you cannot force friendships. What you can do is ask God to reveal your calling. Then, begin obeying His direction. Like David, you will find the people you need as you pursue the purpose you have been given. I am praying for miracle connections for you! There is a movement happening in the hearts of men worldwide toward godly friendships. You are called to be a part of it! Your Father will not forget you!

4

WARRIOR BROTHERS (DAVID & HIS MIGHTY MEN)

Everyone who was suffering hardship, and everyone who was in debt, and everyone who was discontented gathered to him; and he became captain over them.
—1 Samuel 22:2 (AMP)

What image comes to mind when you think of a warrior? My thoughts immediately go to soldiers in elite military ranks. I imagine a select soldier of discipline, strength, and skill. The warrior in my head is battle-scarred, but he is never battle-weary. He is undoubtedly flawed, but he is also super focused. His very posture speaks to his preparation, and he is ready for the battle ahead. The warrior in my thoughts exudes strength and confidence. This guy was chosen for a reason, and you would feel safe being around him. My imaginary warrior is quite remarkable, but he is not real. He is nothing like the men God sent to David.

David is not the person you would have chosen to be king. He was an unlikely choice, and so were the men whom God had sent to him. They were the leftovers of society. David was initially gifted with men who were projects more than they were warriors. They were more of a threat to themselves than the enemies of Israel.

First Samuel 27:2 tells us David's ragtag ranks swelled to 600 men. These men could not pay their bills, were in distress, and, the Bible says, were *"discontented."* (See 1 Samuel 22:2.) The Hebrew word *mar nephesh* means bitterness of soul. These men had been mistreated by others and had brought much of it upon themselves. David was, by now, a fugitive. He was a "cave dweller," and he had invited thousands of "problems" into the cave with him. Yet out of this unlikely group, some of the fiercest warriors and greatest leaders Israel has ever known would rise. They may not have looked or smelled like anything good, but in the middle of the Judean wilderness, David had the men he needed.

My favorite passage in the Bible just may be 1 Corinthians 1:26–29. I memorized these verses the same year God called me into the ministry. *The Message* paraphrases it in a way that speaks deeply to me:

> *Take a good look, friends, at who you were when you got called into this life. I don't see many of "the brightest and the best" among you, not many influential, not many from high-society families. Isn't it obvious that God deliberately chose men and women that the culture overlooks and exploits and abuses, chose these "nobodies" to expose the*

hollow pretensions of the "somebodies"? That makes it quite clear that none of you can get by with blowing your own horn before God.

This is what was happening early in David's time of hiding from Saul in the wilderness. The people the culture had overlooked—the lowest of society, the nobodies—were gathering around the future king. People of position had too much to risk, but these men had a recklessness that, if tamed, could be greatly used by God. They were up for the fight ahead. David had found his warrior brothers.

RELATABLE SCARS

I was about ten years old when I saw *Jaws*, one of the scariest movies ever (in my opinion). This tale about a giant killer shark scared me straight; I've been a bit afraid of the ocean ever since. I remember fishing with my dad the day after we saw the movie. Logic would state that there are no sharks in southern Illinois, but I sure thought one would attack our Bass Tracker boat that morning! As an adult, I have a new appreciation for this fear-producing film, although I still won't leave the safety of the beach very often!

My favorite scene is when the main characters are talking late into the night, and they begin showing their many scars. Quint, the salty old fisherman, starts the contest by making fun of a small wound that the inexperienced and conservative Mr. Brody is tending to. By comparison, he shows him some missing teeth and says, "This is permanent." Then Quint speaks of a fight in Boston and has the experienced but nerdy Mr. Hooper feel the permanent lump on his head. Quickly, Hooper says, "I got that beat," and he shows a large scar on his arm where a moray eel bit through his wetsuit. Next is a mangled arm from Quint's wrestling days, followed by scars left from shark bites.

The scene gets dark at the end of the "contest" as Quint tells of his time in the navy. He speaks of a Japanese torpedo sinking the ship he was serving on. He says, "1,100 men went in the water, but only 316 came out." He relives the nightmare of sharks hunting these floating sailors for five days. The scene is riveting but isn't relatable for most people. My favorite part of these few minutes of cinematic gold is when the inexperienced Mr. Brody does something that is hardly noticed. As the men are showing the history of their injuries, Brody starts to show the scar from his appendix surgery. Before they can see it, he quickly lowers his shirt and opts out of the contest. He thinks he has nothing to show, so he has nothing to say.

I believe I know how Mr. Brody felt. Years ago, I accidentally became a part of a "scar-showing contest" at a men's conference where I was speaking. In the church lobby, I engaged in an enjoyable conversation with several older men. Out of nowhere, they started showing their scars. Each one had a story and a wound that was greater than the next man's. Then it was my turn. They could see I had nothing to show, so they went around the circle again. It was like the scene from *Jaws*. These men had been through some trying circumstances, and they had the wounds to prove it. Before I knew it, they were back to me for a second time, and I still had nothing. After a few awkward moments, the conversation mercifully fizzled out. I knew what had happened, but I was not insecure or embarrassed. My injuries may not have been impressive or even visible, but I had deep scars that they couldn't see—and so do you.

Warriors relate to wounds. It is never our perfection that draws us to each other. No one can relate to that. Our scars always make the best stories and draw the biggest crowds. A part of David's popularity was his relatability. Everyone in Israel would have heard a version of David's story. The men gathering to David would know of his exploits, but they also knew of his predicament. David was in violation of the law of King Saul, no matter how unjust it was. Although his anointing was strong, it was now mixed with hurt and confusion. Somehow, this mixture of pain and purpose became a beacon that drew the right people to him.

David's life at this point reminds me of a glow stick. Glow sticks work when you bend them to the point that a chemical reaction creates light or luminescence. David's brokenness mixed with his anointing and caused a reaction that lit up the cave where he was hiding. Others were attracted to his light, whether he wanted the company or not. He may have wanted to be alone and hide, but these men were willing to do the same. "Soon his brothers and all his other relatives joined him there" (1 Samuel 22:1). Even David's family, the same people who forgot him and belittled him, were coming to light. In the past, his victories may have impressed many, but now his scars were drawing people to his side.

This whole scene has stirred a couple of verses from the book of Revelation in my mind and spirit. John the revelator is repeating what he is seeing and hearing when he writes these warrior words:

> *Then I heard a loud voice in heaven say: "Now have come the salvation and the power and the kingdom of our God, and the authority of his Messiah. For the accuser of our brothers and sisters, who accuses them before our God day and night, has been hurled down. They triumphed over him*

> *by the blood of the Lamb and by the word of their testimony; they did not love their lives so much as to shrink from death."* (Revelation 12:10–11 NIV)

We all are being falsely accused right now, just like David was. This verse says that day and night the *"accuser of our brothers"* is doing what he does best: making accusations. But, prophetically, John sees how he is being defeated: *"by the blood of the Lamb and by the word of their testimony."*

Right there in the cave you are in today, you have two secret weapons. You have the blood of the Lamb and the word of your testimony. You have what Jesus has already done for you and the confidence that He will continue to rescue you. You are going through a test, but the test will end in a testimony. In your broken but redeemed state, right there in your loneliness, like David, you will find people being drawn to join you in your battle. Your brokenness is a beacon.

BEING A "DANGEROUS" BROTHERHOOD

One of my favorite stories to read is that of a lone soldier. Maybe a single warrior is left behind or dropped into hostile territory. He might become a one-man army fighting against the greatest of odds. This narrative seems to speak to the "loner nature" that exists in most men. It certainly exists in me. Now, while there are rare historical cases of individual soldiers making a significant impact, these accounts lack the dramatic effects seen in Hollywood. Characters like Rambo exist only in the movies.

The truth is, being alone makes you far less dangerous. Self-preservation is exhausting when you have no one to watch your back. When you face overwhelming odds, a band of brothers raises your courage and effectiveness exponentially. This is what the initial wave of David's future mighty men did for him. Not only did the presence of these men provide much-needed camaraderie—they brought more "ammunition." This rise in potential came with equal problems, but this goes with the territory of training warriors. Although unformed, the fighting capacity of David's newfound force was enormous.

One of the things that makes brotherhood so dangerous is the motivation it provides. No one uses the attraction of this better than the US military. I read an article dedicated to combat veterans that described it this way: "There is a calling that draws people together, where they are able to establish an environment that breeds the brotherhood that has been sought in every corner of one's life. Upon signing the dotted line, and reserving a place among the world's most elite fighting force, one enters into the unparalleled brotherhood that is the United States military."[12] Even people who have never served are drawn to the power of brotherhood. Brotherhood is a military motivation and should be one of ours, too.

By the time the future mighty men came to the cave, David had been alone for a while. In 1 Samuel 21:1–3, he was alone and running from King Saul when he asked Ahimelech, the priest, for something to eat. He spoke of "his men" when discussing the food, but we are given no details. We know from the psalms he wrote during this time that he was in constant danger and loneliness. David cried, *"My soul is among lions; I lie among the sons of men who are set on fire, whose teeth are spears and arrows, and their tongue a sharp sword"* (Psalm 57:4 NKJV). In another psalm, he cried from the cave, *"Look on my right hand and see, for there is*

---
12. "As Defined in the Military: 'Brotherhood,'" Combat Veterans to Careers, accessed December 23, 2024, https://combatveteranstocareers.org/as-defined-in-the-military-brotherhood/.

YOU HAVE WHAT JESUS HAS ALREADY DONE FOR YOU AND THE CONFIDENCE THAT HE WILL CONTINUE TO RESCUE YOU. YOU ARE GOING THROUGH A TEST, BUT THE TEST WILL END IN A TESTIMONY.

no one who acknowledges me; refuge has failed me; no one cares for my soul" (Psalm 142:4 NKJV). From my study of his timelines, this season of aloneness may have lasted as long as two years. I can only imagine the courage it took to be productive during this isolated season. God used it to form David, but we are not meant to stay in lonely caves forever.

Once David was backed by an army, he became productive on a whole new level. Even with King Saul trying to kill him, David and his men bravely fought the battles of Israel. One of the first battles took place in a town under attack called Keilah.

> *David asked the LORD, "Should I go and attack them?" "Yes, go and save Keilah," the LORD told him. But David's men said, "We're afraid even here in Judah. We certainly don't want to go to Keilah to fight the whole Philistine army!" So David asked the LORD again, and again the LORD replied, "Go down to Keilah, for I will help you conquer the Philistines." So David and his men went to Keilah. They slaughtered the Philistines.* (1 Samuel 23:2–5)

Unlike Saul, David did not placate his men or bow to their fears. Instead, he called them to a higher level and pushed them to obey God. We can only imagine the bonds created in these early victories, the stories that only they could tell. This is how brotherhood is formed. This is how men become dangerous.

As I think of the warrior brothers in my own life, I am struck with the realization that this is the largest category of powerful relationships a man will ever have. Warrior friendships are where we have the most relational room. All it takes to have a warrior brother is to share a common godly goal and a few mutually experienced victories. A brotherhood is forged once you have been together in the fire of battle. I think of the hundreds of men I have built houses and churches with in some of the world's poorest environments—they are my warrior brothers. I've faced challenges with the groups I've traveled with, like being trapped in Ecuador due to a strike and getting stuck on a mountain in Burundi. These experiences have forged our bonds and made us brothers.

This kind of fusion demands danger. It is only in times of conflict that armies are truly formed. Every man needs to be a part of something like this. The details may be different, and you may not have to get on a plane to find your common cause. But you must have a mission bigger than you can handle on your own. You will never find your brothers while you remain in the cave by yourself.

NAVIGATE BROTHERLY COMPLICATIONS

When I hear the word "brother," I do not always think of the military or the men's ministry at my church. Those are both rich and true expressions of a warrior connection, but they are not my only experience with brotherhood. Many of us grew up in a house with a brother or brothers. I have an older brother whom I both admired and feared. He could affirm me or torture me, sometimes both in the same minute! No one can find your weaknesses and exploit them like a brother. No one can more fiercely protect you than your brother. Brothers are a two-edged sword that can kill the enemy or cut you wide open. In this early season of his life, David experienced both from his developing group of elite men.

> *David kept thinking to himself, "Someday Saul is going to get me. The best thing I can do is escape to the Philistines. Then Saul will stop hunting for me in Israelite territory,*

and I will finally be safe." So David took his 600 men and went over and joined Achish son of Maoch, the king of Gath. David and his men and their families settled there with Achish at Gath. (1 Samuel 27:1–3)

Did you catch the opening verse? It does not say "David prayed," as we have seen so many other times. It says, *"David kept thinking to himself...."* What did David think? He thought that his men, their families, and he and his family should all go live in the land of the Philistines. This is so crazy because it is the land where Goliath hailed from—the land of his enemy, an enemy who has sworn to kill David. This was not a good plan; this was a mistake. God showed him grace and preserved His servant, but not before there were king-sized complications.

At this stage of his story, David entered into a strange and deceitful alliance with a Philistine ruler named Achish. He and his men were still raiding and destroying Philistine towns and territories, but David regularly deceived Achish about it. (See 1 Samuel 27:8–12.) God protected him and gave him favor despite his dishonesty. This insanity all culminates in 1 Samuel 29 when Achish wants David and his men to go with the Philistine army and fight against Israel. Achish's own commanders rightfully did not trust David and protested until he had to tell David and his men they couldn't be a part of their army. You can imagine the confusion all of this caused among David's men. But these warrior brothers stuck with David, at least until 1 Samuel 30. This is where David's warrior brothers became a threat to David himself.

While David and his men were off with the Philistine army, their temporary hometown of Ziklag was raided by the Amalekites. *"They found that the Amalekites had made a raid into the Negev and Ziklag; they had crushed Ziklag and burned it to the ground. They had carried off the women and children and everyone else but without killing anyone*" (1 Samuel 30:1–2). David's failure in leadership created deep bitterness and anger in his men, so much so that they wanted to stone him to death. The men "*wept until they could weep no more*" (1 Samuel 30:4). The Amalekite raid and David's decisions had brought the men to intense despair.

What did David do? David did what we will see him do in all the lowest moments of his life. When he fails in character or in leadership, we always see David run back to the figurative cave where he can talk to his heavenly Father. "*David found strength in the LORD his God*" (1 Samuel 30:6). In the following verses, we see David seeking God with the help of Abiathar, the priest. I believe this was done in front of his men. This highlights the complex tension of brotherhood that comes with humbling oneself before God and others, which is what David did.

The Lord answered David's cries and gave him direction to go after the Amalekites. They got back everything that was taken, every man, woman, and child and every item. (See 1 Samuel 30:17–20.) The true leader, David, was back, and his men knew it. Sometimes, God allows a flood of complications to carry us back to a place of reliance on Him. I believe that David's stature was raised here by his response to this failure—even more than all his victories combined. True warrior brotherhood flourishes when we navigate disasters together. Every one of David's men had failed before. Now, they saw their future king do the same. This brick of humility became the foundational piece of David's future leadership. This is how brotherhood flourishes.

AVOID SILLY SELFISHNESS

I was recently fishing with a friend in my small boat when his lure got caught on brush near a dam. As I backed up to free the line, my trolling motor bumped against some submerged rocks, and we suddenly lost power. I used my emergency paddle to get back to the boat ramp, but we couldn't determine the issue. I later discovered that an inline fuse on the wires leading to the front of my boat had blown. Once I replaced it, everything worked fine. The motor getting stuck had caused a power surge that triggered the fuse.

Leaders sometimes must act like the fuse did in my boat. They must halt disaster by performing a corrective action. This is never fun, but it is a part of being a warrior brother. In 1 Samuel 30, David and his men were barely back on track when they started bumping against the rocks of poor character. First Samuel 30:9–10 tells us, *"David and his 600 men set out, and they came to the brook Besor. But 200 of the men were too exhausted to cross the brook, so David continued the pursuit with 400 men."* So, two hundred of David's men were so exhausted that they stayed behind on the other side of the brook. The remaining four hundred experienced an overwhelming victory over the Amalekites. Everyone's family was rescued, and there was an abundance of plunder. This should've been a great day all around, but petty selfishness started to appear from some of the men. *"Some evil troublemakers among David's men said, 'They didn't go with us, so they can't have any of the plunder we recovered. Give them their wives and children, and tell them to be gone"* (1 Samuel 30:22).

Nothing kills brotherhood faster than selfishness. The very nature of being a warrior brother is that you are for others, not for yourself. The moment you start "keeping score" is the moment you stop being sacrificial. I am so glad Jesus does not

NOTHING KILLS BROTHERHOOD
FASTER THAN SELFISHNESS.
THE VERY NATURE OF BEING A
WARRIOR BROTHER
IS THAT YOU ARE FOR OTHERS,
NOT FOR YOURSELF.

do this with us! Jesus was the ultimate warrior brother because everything He did was for us. Jesus said, *"Greater love hath no man than this, that a man lay down his life for his friends"* (John 15:13 KJV). This is the very essence of being a warrior brother. Brotherhood is a willingness to lose so others can win.

What I hate the most about the pettiness of these men is the message they sent. "You only get what we have, where we are, if you earn it," they were saying. This is anti-grace and anti-generosity. The goal of any successful godly man should be to bless other men with what he has. You want to take the "two hundred" to where you are, not send them away to be stuck where they are. If you have the strength for battle, then your calling is to lift the exhausted, not punish them for being worn out. "No man left behind" is the mantra of all true warrior brothers. These selfish men needed to correct their motivation. They needed to be led.

One of my warrior brothers (and spiritual sons) is a friend named Jake. He is one of the men who travels often with me on my missions work, especially in Africa. Jake has a vast resume of his own, and I always feel safer when he is with me. A few years ago, our team was traveling through Addis Ababa, Ethiopia. We had a quick connection at the airport, and all of us were exhausted. Although I was the most experienced traveler, I was separated from the group and boarded a different bus. This started a chain reaction that put me half an hour behind everyone else. I was going to miss our flight, and my delay could last for days.

It was futile, but I decided to run, just in case I could possibly make it. As I approached the gate, all I could see was my warrior brother Jake and a bunch of angry-looking airline employees. Jake had held up the plane, delaying hundreds of people, so I would make it. He risked getting back to his own family so I could get back to mine. A combination of relief and personal depletion caused me to burst into tears as I boarded the plane. I have since returned the favor to Jake, but he never required that. Holding up planes so everyone can board is just something warrior brothers do.

For whom are you holding up the plane? How many undeserving men are you blessing with the victories you have experienced? Who's going with you on your warrior journey? I think this is why David blew a fuse. The situation with his men went so starkly against kingdom principles and true warrior philosophy. The disunity caused by selfishness would have been a poison that slowly but surely destroyed David's growing army.

> *David said, "No, my brothers! Don't be selfish with what the LORD has given us. He has kept us safe and helped us defeat the band of raiders that attacked us. Who will listen when you talk like this? We share and share alike—those who go to battle and those who guard the equipment." From then on, David made this a decree and regulation for Israel, and it is still followed today.* (1 Samuel 30:23–25)

What a moment this was. David reestablished his leadership, affirmed his weaker forces, and corrected bad-spirited men—all at the same time. David reminded the men who they really were. They were warriors, and the 200 were their brothers. David's strong leadership that day saved a third of his army and forged a warrior bond among them that they would need for the coming battles.

Remember the lesson of the almost-banished 200 as you begin to form your own army of warrior brothers. Including the forgotten ones is how you will grow your ranks. Using your success to bless those who do not possess your strength will attract other warriors to your battles. Decide today that you will reject the separation that comes from silly selfishness. Be a generous warrior. Open your world like this, and you will never have to fight your battles alone.

5

BRAVE PARTNERS (DAVID & ABISHAI)

Taking charge, David spoke to Ahimelech the Hittite and to Abishai son of Zeruiah, Joab's brother: "Who will go down with me and enter Sau"s camp?" Abishai whispered, "I'll go with you."
—1 Samuel 26:6 (MSG)

Let's start this chapter with a powerful mental exercise. I want you to think about something God has called you to accomplish. Mentally access the shelf of unfinished dreams in your mind and select the one that has been your biggest nemesis. That dream will take genuine miracles to perform. Cognitively place it in the middle of an imaginary empty field. In your mind, start surrounding your dream with obstacles in the form of enemy warriors. Make them mean, scary, and big. Imagine that your enemies are heavily armed. After mentally making a few mythical warriors, multiply your adversarial force until you reach 3,000. In your conceptualized battlefield, your largest dream should now be surrounded by 3,000 barbarians. They want to kill you and your dream—not a pretty picture.

In chapter two, we discussed how the things God calls us to are constantly surrounded by opposing forces. Most men never even really attempt to get through the opposition. Most men never really touch the big things they are called to. They run away when they should stand and fight. However, you and I are not ordinary men. Neither was David.

The scene in 1 Samuel 26 is much like the field of enemies we just imagined. The story here has so many interesting layers that I almost don't know where to begin. Verse 2 says, *"Saul took 3,000 of Israel's elite troops and went to hunt him down in the wilderness of Ziph."* Saul was more committed than ever to killing David, and he was using Israel's most advanced fighting force to do it. Here is where the story gets good: *"David slipped over to Saul's camp one night to look around. Saul and Abner son of Ner, the commander of his army, were sleeping inside a ring formed by the slumbering warriors"* (1 Samuel 26:5). King Saul, the man who occupied the very role that David was called to, was sleeping in the middle of 3,000 highly skilled warriors. They all had one mission: kill David. If I had been in David's shoes, I might have avoided that situation and explored another wilderness. David did the opposite, but he was not alone.

David asked, *"Who will volunteer to go in there with me?"* (1 Samuel 26:6). Only Abishai spoke up and agreed to go. *"David and Abishai went right into Saul's camp and found him asleep, with his spear stuck in the ground beside his head"* (1 Samuel 26:7).

Just as happened in 1 Samuel 24, David ended up sparing Saul's life, even though Abishai wanted to kill Saul and put an end to David's running. Instead, David took Saul's water jug and spear to prove he could have killed him but would not do it. He later used these items to mock Abner, the leader of Saul's guards, and confront King Saul.

This was not the day David would become king. This was not the moment when David's dream would come to pass. Instead, it was the day he walked past 3,000 soldiers and touched what would be his. How could he do such a thing? Can you imagine what Abishai felt as he joined David in his exploits that day? David multiplied his courage by partnering with an ally. He progressed in a problematic area of his life because someone was brave enough to accompany him. Few people would venture into territory like this for their gain, yet Abishai did it for David. Can you imagine how motivated his men were that night? This moment provided a much-needed break from the relentless pursuit of Saul's army. This moment reminded everyone of David's prophetic calling. It marked the start of a forty-year partnership with Abishai.

Abishai was one of three sons of David's sister Zeruiah. (See 1 Chronicles 2:16.) His brothers were Asahel and Joab, two of David's mighty men whom we will cover in chapter eight. Second Samuel 23:19 tells us: *"Abishai was the most famous of the Thirty and was their commander."* This brave partner of David would eventually become the leader of David's special forces and one of the most accomplished warriors in Israel. Saying yes to a crazy request from his future king would launch Abishai into his God-ordained future.

Moments such as this one between David and Abishai are where partnerships are birthed. Partners are not recruited *by* you; they are raised up *for* you. Brave partners watch and wait for the season they are needed—even if they don't realize it. Someone is waiting for you right now! They may not be on your radar, but they are on God's. He knows how to connect you with your Abishai. The partners God is calling to you will be like the merging of strong forces—like two magnets that cannot be pulled apart. Strengths and weaknesses will be complemented, and visions will be fulfilled. Every man, no matter how gifted he is, needs an Abishai.

Abishai, being related to David, also had a target on his back. Being his nephew, Abishai would have had access to observe David that few others had. He had witnessed David's leadership and could see the anointing on his life. Abishai knew that David was supposed to be king. He was devoted to his giant-killing uncle and was a part of his small fighting force. But it was this crazy moment in 1 Samuel 26 that made him stand out. He rose through the ranks by doing something no one else would do.

What I love about Abishai is how he came into his calling by helping someone else fulfill his. It takes bravery to chase your own lofty goals, but it takes even greater courage to throw in with someone else's extreme ambitions—to trust another's dream. You may know your motives and logic, but how can you know these things in someone else? You may know your heart, but can you trust theirs? Brave partnerships require outstanding audacity, and Abishai had this in abundance.

If you have a significant dream, you will need a partner. If your power and resources can accomplish your dream, it is a small dream indeed. God always calls us to things that are bigger than ourselves. In this, there is faith and extreme dependence on Him. But there is also an undeniable need for others. Your purpose demands partners. The dreams and plans God has placed on your life are interlaced with the gifts, callings, and resources of other people with whom you are connected. It is not your job to define who those people are. Instead, you must courageously enter exploits of faith while you invite others to come with you. For most of us, our partnerships will be few but mighty. If you live on mission for Jesus, brave partners will be one of the greatest weapons in your arsenal. They will be the catalysts that maximize every gift you have been given.

PARTNERSHIP POTENTIAL

Your ability to partner with others will largely determine your potential. This is true no matter how gifted you are. So, we must ask ourselves: "How can I raise my partnership potential?" This is a question I ask myself almost every day. The name of our ministry is Partnership Ministries, and we are dedicated to partnership. Our missions initiative, Partnership International, serves as our means of collaborating with ministries in some of the world's poorest regions to create a meaningful impact. We maintain close connections with our "partner churches" and foster relationships with our "partnership network" of individuals who support our mission.

Even the process of writing this book involves a partnership between the publisher and collaborators. Everything we undertake is centered around partnership. Our success depends on developing strong, lasting partnerships with those who share the mission that God has given us. I pray every day that God will help us expand our partnerships.

Partnerships at the kingdom level, like the partnership between David and Abishai, are divine gifts from God. They cannot be formed solely through our efforts; that would be risky. You are gambling with your calling if you are not selective

PARTNERS ARE NOT RECRUITED *BY* YOU; THEY ARE RAISED UP *FOR* YOU. BRAVE PARTNERS WATCH AND WAIT FOR THE SEASON THEY ARE NEEDED— EVEN IF THEY DON'T REALIZE IT.

in your partnerships. Alone, we may choose the wrong people and create ineffective relationships or jeopardize everything we've worked for.

So, I enter this section with caution. I believe steps can be taken to add God-given attractiveness to your life and calling. There are some relational best practices when it comes to partnerships. As we choose to partner with people, we must never forget to honor the Holy Spirit and *"let the peace that comes from Christ rule your* [our] *hearts"* (Colossians 3:15).

I have made four major commitments that I believe increase the favor and wisdom of God in my life in the area of partnerships.

FIRST, I PRIORITIZE PARTNERING WITH OTHERS' NEEDS BEFORE REQUESTING MY OWN.

This is the *"do unto others"* (Luke 6:31 MEV) biblical mandate in action. If you want God to do something for you, start doing that very thing for other people. Make the dreams of others come true, and you will increase God's favor for your Spirit-led ambitions. I am "Abishai" for several people in my life. I refuse to let my spiritual leaders fight alone. I will be the first to volunteer when they need to sneak into the enemy's camp. I give generously to other causes and ministries beyond my own. I counsel and contend with those I partner with so that I may help their kingdom dreams come true. I do for others what I hope God will do for me.

SECOND, I AM WILLING TO COMMIT EVEN WHEN I DO NOT FULLY UNDERSTAND.

Leaders are visionary people. By their very nature, visions do not come with every detail attached. God will show us a broad picture and then fill in the details as we obey Him. This makes me think of David's friend Jonathan and his armor-bearer in 1 Samuel 14. Long before David met his covenant friend, Jonathan faced a moment similar to David's facing Goliath. No wonder they had such a connection. Jonathan went up against a Philistine army that no one else was willing to fight. His brave partner that day was his young armor-bearer. He asked him to go with him and attack an entire force, just the two of them. Crazy, right?

Look at the way Jonathan invited the guy who carried his stuff to go with him: *"'Let's go across to the outpost of those pagans,' Jonathan said to his armor bearer. 'Perhaps the L*ORD *will help us, for nothing can hinder the L*ORD*. He can win a battle whether he has many warriors or only a few!'"* (1 Samuel 14:6). Jonathan proposed that two guys fight a whole division of the Philistine army, and all he told his armor-bearer was, *"Perhaps the L*ORD *will help us."* I would want some more details! But brave partners move with the hearts of their leaders. They value inspiration even over information. That is what Jonathan's armor-bearer did, and a great victory was won that day. Partnerships are powerful.

THIRD, I LOOK FOR PEOPLE WHO HAVE A SIMILAR MISSION AND EQUAL PASSION.

There is no sense in partnering with someone whose mission is flowing in an opposite direction from mine. I bless all, but I partner with few. I also am very sensitive to someone whose passion is waning, especially if they have developed a bitter spirit. I can help hurting people but cannot place them on the frontlines of my battle. You have potential partners when you find people with the same mission who maintain the purity of their passion. Be selective! God has not called you to everybody. Some partnerships will not last a lifetime, like Abishai's did with David. Some people are booster rockets. They are supposed to help you get off the ground but are not called to your mission long-term.

FINALLY, I AM COMMITTED TO PROTECTING THOSE I PARTNER WITH.

There is protection in partnership. On the board of my ministry, I have four people who fill the role of Abishai. Actually, we have five; I am an Abishai to each of them, as well. We protect each other in several ways. There is a high level of accountability that protects both me and our organization. But it's deeper than that. The insight and wisdom we have for each other help us avoid a thousand pitfalls. Even further, we are willing to fight for each other and even take "hits" ourselves if it will protect both the mission and the person. This harkens back to my first point about "doing unto others" what you want God to do for you. Abishai would become a direct protector of David, putting himself in harm's way repeatedly for his leader and king. You are vulnerable if you do not have someone like that in your life. We all need protectors; we all need an Abishai.

Let me share a bonus principle here: *the principle of prayer*. This should be the very foundation of partnership. I mentioned in the introduction that we should not pray for resources as much as we should pray for relationships. I do my best not to pray for money because I know that where there is a God-ordained mission, there will be God-given provision. The great missionary Hudson Taylor said, "God's work done in God's way will never lack God's supply." So, a superior strategy to our resource-laced repetitions in prayer is to ask God for an expansion in kingdom partnerships. God typically provides through people. The most likely source of provision will be the partnerships He sends your way. This is why we should pray. All good things come from Him.

PARTNERSHIP PROBLEMS

You have probably heard some version of this story: A man is shipwrecked on an island or maybe stuck on the roof of his house during a flood. He prays for God to rescue him, and a boat comes, but he tells the captain of the boat, "I am waiting on God." A helicopter and a plane attempt to rescue him, but he gives the same reply to each of these. The man dies in his waiting and stands before God with his complaint, "Why didn't You rescue me, God?" God replies, "I sent a boat, a plane, and a helicopter." The man rejected the rescue because the form in which they came was not what he expected. Partnerships rarely come in perfect packages. They are often in forms we are not expecting, and they carry challenges we would like to avoid.

About a decade ago, I was experiencing some big problems around partnerships. It seemed like every Abishai in my life was more of a discipleship project than a protector and promoter of the mission God had given me. I had developed a cautious attitude that was killing my desire for camaraderie. This led me to a season where I was still sneaking into Saul's camp, but I was doing it by myself and did not ask for a partner. Exhaustion was setting in as my friendships were wearing thin.

This season culminated with a meeting I had with a partner we had been serving with for quite a while. He had been exhibiting character issues that made working together difficult. None of these issues was insurmountable, but they required more relational effort than I wanted to give. As I was about to meet with this person, I clearly heard God say to my spirit, "All partnerships are with people, and people are never perfect." At that moment, I began to repent, and God put a heart of graceful mentorship inside me toward my partner. Our meeting included some corrections, but there was a spirit of humility coming out of me that preserved the partnership. To this day, we are still working together. All partnerships are mixed with problems that should be prayerfully, gracefully, and thoughtfully brought to a solution.

Abishai was a physically strong man, and I think he had a personality to match. We know that when David took Saul's spear, he had to talk Abishai down, or he would have killed Saul: *"'God has surely handed your enemy over to you this time!' Abishai whispered to David. 'Let me pin him to the ground with one thrust of the spear; I won't need to strike twice!'"* (1 Samuel 26:8). David patiently whispered to him about godly restraint, and Abishai submitted. It would have been great if Abishai's partnership with David had remained clean so we could focus on his heroic exploits. Conflicts can create confusion. The key is to run with our responsibilities but to add a lot of grace to our fast pace. We should never make our goals more important than the people we work with. Colossians 3:13 says, *"Make allowance for each other's faults, and forgive anyone who offends you. Remember, the Lord forgave you, so you must forgive others."* This attitude of forbearance is required if you are going to have lasting partnerships.

The massive need for relational grace is on full display during David's transition to the throne. Kingly transitions are extremely dangerous because kingdoms are vulnerable before leadership is established. Chapters 2 and 3 of 2 Samuel are a messy, mixed bag of conflicts as the kingdoms of Judah and Israel are in transition. David becomes the king of Judah,

ALL PARTNERSHIPS ARE MIXED WITH PROBLEMS THAT SHOULD BE PRAYERFULLY, GRACEFULLY, AND THOUGHTFULLY BROUGHT TO A SOLUTION.

and the royal calling on his life is underway. (See 2 Samuel 2:1–6.) Abner tries to avoid a fight with Asahel, but he does not relent, and Abner ends up killing him. (See 2 Samuel 2:18–23.)

Abner is then slain by Abishai and his brother Joab in revenge for Asahel's death. (See 2 Samuel 3:22–30.) The killing of Abner, Saul's former commander, was a difficult blow for David. Abner had completed an alliance with David before his demise and was also consulting with the elders of Israel to make David king. This frustrated David so much that he rebuked his two closest men:

> *Even though I am the anointed king, these two sons of Zeruiah—Joab and Abishai—are too strong for me to control. So may the LORD repay these evil men for their evil deeds.* (2 Samuel 3:39)

In a fury of frustration, David declared Abishai and Joab to be out of control, and he even called them *"evil men."* This declaration was not factual, even though, at that moment, their actions were sinful and unwise. From future studies, we know that David would not break off his relationship with these flawed yet amazing men. They would become even more essential to David and his kingdom. David would cautiously operate in relational grace.

Partnerships can be complicated. Destinies are messy, especially royal ones. This is the two-edged sword of powerful partnerships. Partners are essential, but when people are involved, challenges are inevitable. Will your frustration turn you into a destroyer of people, or will it make you a preserver of partnerships?

GIANT SLAYERS

Every year, I have an opportunity to hunt deer in central Illinois. It is a large property with lots of set-up stands to choose from, and your chances of bagging a nice-sized deer are pretty good. I have grown kind of lazy in my outdoor pursuits over the years, so my favorite places to hunt on the property are the closed-in raised box blinds. They are situated in key locations, and we have little gas-powered heaters that make the cold days much more bearable. The blinds sit there untouched until fall, so they are home to some insects in the warmer months.

For some reason, there are always a few dead flies around the window trim of the blinds. During my first year hunting from one of these, I noticed something kind of scary about the flies. After the blind would warm up, some of the flies would come back to life—like a zombie! I researched this phenomenon; the flies are actually in a hibernation-like state, and they can recover for a brief while and live again. This is the stuff of horror movies, but I saw it with my eyes.

In 2 Samuel 21, King David has what must have felt like a "zombie giant" moment. The Bible tells us that David and his men were once again fighting the Philistines. David was not as young as he used to be, and he became extremely exhausted from the battle. (See 2 Samuel 21:15.) The next verse says, *"Ishbi-benob was a descendant of the giants; his bronze spearhead weighed more than seven pounds, and he was armed with a new sword. He had cornered David and was about to kill him"* (2 Samuel 21:16). Sound familiar? This guy looked like Goliath and was carrying weapons similar to those Goliath wielded. Even more, this guy was related to Goliath—the giant was back! There were actually four giants on the battlefield that day, all of them from the same place as Goliath. (See 2 Samuel 21:22.) They had their hands full! This time, David was not the energetic teenager he once was; he was physically and emotionally exhausted. He was on the verge of being defeated by a giant and urgently needed help.

Who swooped in to save the day? His brave partner, Abishai! *"Abishai son of Zeruiah came to David's rescue and killed the Philistine"* (2 Samuel 21:17). The men were so moved when they realized they had almost lost their king that they declared to David, *"You are not going out to battle with us again! Why risk snuffing out the light of Israel?"* (verse 17). So, in his bone-weary state, David was rescued by a partnership that many leaders would have broken off eighteen chapters earlier. You could say with accuracy that it was the longevity of his partnership that provided his protection.

The grace required to preserve the relationship with Abishai actually saved David's life. You may not realize you need others today, but one day, you will be surrounded, like David was. On that day, it will be the legacy of your relationships that saves you. Some of these partnerships will have lasted a lifetime. These will be the richest and most protective relationships you will ever have. Without an Abishai (or several), all of us would be doomed because the giants would never stop coming.

SHARED VICTORIES

I am going to take a guess and say that you have a Bible somewhere nearby. As I write this, I am in my office, with probably twenty copies of a Bible on my nearby shelf (not to mention the electronic versions installed on my phone and computer). English-speaking people have easy access to God's life-giving Word. This has not always been the case. We owe a debt of gratitude to many who gave their very lives so we could read and be changed by the Word of God. One of those people was

William Tyndale, an influential figure during the Protestant Reformation.

In the past, if you wanted to read the Bible but didn't know Latin, you were out of luck. Even if you understood Latin, the Bible was often chained to the pulpit of your local church, meaning only the priests could read it. The common people did not have access to the Scriptures in their own language.

Tyndale was a gifted linguist who knew Greek, Hebrew, and Latin. He would become one of the greatest Bible translators to ever live. His work was so accurate that most of the King James Bible was taken from his work. However, there is a footnote in history that most people will miss when it comes to the work of William Tyndale. In his revolutionary book called *Gospel Patrons*, author John Rinehart tells the story of Tyndale's brave partner, Humphrey Monmouth. He was a merchant who helped Tyndale with not only resources but also a place to live and, ultimately, a way to distribute the first copies of Scripture.[13] The Bible you are reading today is available to you partially due to a divine partnership between two unlikely men. Everything great in God's kingdom happens in partnership.

A patron is defined as "one that uses wealth or influence to help an individual, an institution, or a cause."[14] This term is a useful reference for those called to a mission who wonder why God doesn't simply provide the financial support needed. God doesn't operate that way. Instead, He meshes callings together in the form of partnerships. Your mission may be the very platform someone else needs to fulfill the calling God placed on their life. Just like Tyndale needed Monmouth, you need some-

---

13. John Rinehart, *Gospel Patrons: People Whose Generosity Changed the World* (CreateSpace Publishing, 2014), 34–55.
14. *Merriam-Webster.com Dictionary*, s.v. "patron, accessed January 2, 2025, https://www.merriam-webster.com/dictionary/patron. Accessed 2 Jan. 2025.

one, too. The victory God wants to bring through you is meant to be shared.

When I teach this truth in churches, I often point to the pastor and say, "Every preacher needs a patron." This is not an attempt to raise money, but it is a prophetic call toward those who are gifted to use their support and influence for that church and pastor. Whatever victories a pastor and their church achieve are meant to be shared. In fact, there are people in every church who are actually gifted by God to finance the work of the gospel. Among the spiritual gifts listed in Romans 12 is to *"give generously"* (verse 8). Paul writes in 2 Corinthians 8:7 that we should *"excel also in this gracious act of giving."* Some people are graced to give—it is the very calling God placed on them. The greatest things happen when someone gifted with ministry unites with someone gifted with giving—this is a partnership at its best.

I pray that this chapter will create a river that flows in two directions. I pray that partners will emerge out of the chaos of your commitment to follow the ambitions God has placed on your heart. I also pray that you will be the answer to someone else's prayer for partnership. Only in stepping into this dual flow of this river of kingdom collaboration can we see all the purposes of God accomplished through us. Our hopes for success are connected to each other.

If you read further about Abishai, you will find that he once killed 300 enemies using only his spear. (See 1 Chronicles 11:20.) He also led a campaign that defeated 18,000 other enemies who wanted to destroy Israel. (See 1 Chronicles 18:12.) His individual battle accomplishments may have been even greater than those of King David himself. He would lead David's most elite soldiers and would be loyal to the king to the day of his death. Abishai was so interlaced with the success of David that we will never know his full impact on this side of heaven. His partnership with the man we are studying is a testament to the fact that none of us succeeds alone. When God raises up a David, He always raises up an Abishai. All our victories are shared—true for kings and true for you and me.

6

SPIRITUAL SONS
(DAVID & MEPHIBOSHETH)

> *From that time on, Mephibosheth ate regularly at David's table, like one of the king's own sons.*
> —2 Samuel 9:11

There are certain dramatic themes that naturally repeat themselves in literature and film. These narratives persist because they speak our souls: a hero on a mission, a victim in need of rescue, a man overcoming his weakness, or a failure seeking redemption. One of the frequent repetitive plots we see is that of a son in desperate need of a father. The son is a gifted but lost soul who has a measure of success but is struggling with abandonment. His fatherless state has left him drifting and searching. Then, somehow, a surrogate father appears, and a relationship ensues.

This father figure answers the son's questions with wisdom and direction—but his noble work is much deeper.

It's like his fatherly role bridges a gap in the manhood of his son that could not be fixed without his help. This relationship is usually not the main subject of the movie or book, but it is typically the part that resonates with us the most. This theme is so common because the necessity is so universal. We are all sons who need fathers.

This inherent instinct is a two-sided coin. On one side is the need, and on the other is the responsibility. We certainly are sons in need of fathers, but we are also fathers in need of sons. This fatherly mission extends beyond biology. As I wrote earlier, part of being a man of God is an intentional willingness to adopt spiritual sons. This is the great biblical theme: Moses had Joshua, Elijah had Elisha, Paul had Timothy, and David became a father to a broken young man named Mephibosheth. His name is not nearly as complicated to say as his story is to tell.

Mephibosheth was a royal son from a regime everyone was trying to forget. His very existence was a lingering reminder of a humiliated dynasty. He was the grandson of former King Saul and the son of David's deceased best friend, Jonathan. Mephibosheth could have made the case that he should be king—he was just a couple of heartbeats away from the throne—but the whole world had moved on from that possibility. To make matters worse, Mephibosheth had sustained a physical injury that had left him permanently disabled.

Second Samuel 4:4 says:

Saul's son Jonathan had a son named Mephibosheth, who was crippled as a child. He was five years old when the report came from Jezreel that Saul and Jonathan had been killed in battle. When the child's nurse heard the news, she picked him up and fled. But as she hurried away, she dropped him, and he became crippled.

In the danger of the moment, Mephibosheth became a victim of his grandfather's sins. He was thrust into fatherlessness, severely injured, and in fear of what the new regime would do. Most newly crowned kings probably would have had him killed, but David was no ordinary king.

This part of David's account is the first time we see him at peace. David was not on the run when he initiated his relationship with Mephibosheth. Instead, David did so as the undisputed and unchallenged king. Second Samuel 3:1 tells us that there was a *"long war between those who were loyal to Saul and those loyal to David. As time passed David became stronger and stronger, while Saul's dynasty became weaker and weaker."* David was now in charge of all of Israel and was stacking up military victories. Peace and prosperity grew under David's rule, and God's promises were fulfilled before his eyes.

Right about the time most kings would have rested, David made this extraordinary request: *"Is anyone in Saul's family still alive—anyone to whom I can show kindness for Jonathan's sake?"* (2 Samuel 9:1). With honor in his heart and his long-lost friend on his mind, King David sought to bless someone from the former royal family. This was extremely unusual for several reasons. This kind of intention from David went completely against the usual nature of monarchies. When a new king was established, it was customary to wipe out the lineage of the former ruling family. Not only was David breaking protocol, but he was seeking to bless his predecessor.

We also have to consider that King Saul spent the last decade of his life trying to kill David. That alone would move many men toward revenge or at least to ignore the former royal family. For David to have a blessing in his heart was unprecedented. His lack of insecurity was astounding, and his generosity could even have been interpreted as foolishness by some.

Another barrier that David blew past was the fact that he was not from a royal family. His only royal relationship came through his marriage to Saul's daughter. This was a weak case compared to others who were direct descendants of Israel's former king. David should've made his throne more secure by killing off Saul's family, not extending his power to help them. But self-promotion and self-preservation were never the way of this unlikely king. This former shepherd boy let benevolence reign over insecurity, and he would be rewarded for it. He would gain a son.

LONELY LO-DEBAR

> *"Are you Ziba?" the king asked. "Yes sir, I am," Ziba replied. The king then asked him, "Is anyone still alive from Saul's family? If so, I want to show God's kindness to them." Ziba replied, "Yes, one of Jonathan's sons is still alive. He is crippled in both feet." "Where is he?" the king asked. "In Lo-debar," Ziba told him.* (2 Samuel 9:2–4)

Theologians often point out the beautiful similarities among redemptive themes throughout the Scriptures as compared to the redemption story of Jesus, seeking "types," or symbols, of Christ. In this account, David is a "type" of Christ as he seeks to "save" someone who does not deserve it. Mephibosheth is a "type" of you and me; his "rescue" models our own need to be saved. Also, Ziba becomes an (imperfect) "type" of the Holy Spirit as he seeks out Mephibosheth and brings him to David.

Ziba's answer to the king's question in verse 3 is so telling. He has not even given David a name yet, and he has already announced that Mephibosheth is disabled in both feet. He leads with the boy's broken condition because that is all he really sees. This former grandson of the king has an injury that has become his very identity. Ziba is basically saying, "You don't really want this one; he isn't the kind of person you should associate with." This is usually the case with potential spiritual sons. They are marred by their history, and their stories are webs you can get caught in yourself. Ziba's not-so-subtle warning did not stop David. Fathers have to embrace the complications or they will never find a son.

Ziba tells the King that Mephibosheth is in a place called Lo-Debar. The word is a geographical term referring to a town located in the region of Gilead. Lo-Debar means "no pasture," "nothing," or "pastureless."[15] What do they do with a boy who is a part of the leftovers of an embarrassing regime? They put him in a barren place because no one will look for him there. They put him in a barren, isolated land because no one wants to be reminded of what he represents. Mephibosheth went from playing in the hallways of the palace to being a nobody from nowhere. As a royal toddler, his every move was chronicled and celebrated, but now he was cursed by the silence of forced anonymity.

Lo-Debar represents the cage of all our broken pasts. It is the place where a person settles into shame and accepts their injuries as an unchangeable identity. We all can end up living

---

15. "Lo Debar," Bible Hub, accessed January 3, 2025, https://biblehub.com/hebrew/3810.htm.

THIS FORMER SHEPHERD BOY
LET BENEVOLENCE REIGN OVER
INSECURITY, AND HE WOULD BE
REWARDED FOR IT. HE WOULD
GAIN A SON.

outside of what God originally intended for us. For most, it is not our circumstances or the abuses of others. It is our own sins and failures that lead us to Lo-Debar. The judgment is self-imposed, and the sentence is long. All it takes is a belief in the lie that you are shameful and should be forgotten. In our day, there are legions of people who have decided to live in a lesser place. They have forgotten who they are.

Lo-Debar is where you will find spiritual sons. All of us fathers who need sons should not waste our time approaching the royal palace to ask if there are any princes who need to be mentored. Those jobs are already taken. In Lo-Debar, you will find an abundance of hidden and hurting men of all ages—men in need of rescue or even just simple recognition. They are not expecting a king to call for them, but they are waiting for someone. We all are. Like Mephibosheth, the life we are meant to have cannot really begin without the blessing that only a father can provide.

I write about fathers and sons from both perspectives because I am a father and a son. I have a wonderful dad, whom I wrote about extensively in my last book, *Divine Intentions*. He taught me grace and instilled a work ethic in me that carries me to this day. I also have been blessed with spiritual fathers who have been assigned to me by God. One of those men was a dear pastor friend named Larry. He passed away a few years ago, and I still miss him very much. When I met Larry, I was in my early thirties and just starting my journey as a traveling evangelist. I was recommended to his church by a friend, but Pastor Larry did not know me. He decided to have me come speak anyway, and I am forever grateful for the relationship it birthed.

I remember sharing in a single service on Sunday morning and another one on Sunday night. Afterward, Larry affirmed me in a deeply authentic way. It was like he saw my gifts and my calling better than I did. That weekend, he asked if we could continue providing services throughout the week. I took a lengthy trip back home to retrieve more clothes but returned and stayed a few more days. That week kicked off a relationship that lasted until his death. It was evident right away that Pastor Larry could speak into my Lo-Debar. There were many areas of barrenness within me, and I had not communicated with anyone about them. Without even realizing it was happening, Larry was leading me out of my wilderness. He became a father to me, and the insight he gave me so freely still speaks to my soul.

We have no record of Mephibosheth praying for a fatherly rescue, but I am certain he prayed for help. I know that I never asked God for a spiritual father, but He absolutely sent one. God has a way to *"turn the hearts of fathers to their children, and the hearts of children to their fathers"* (Malachi 4:6). When spiritual fathers are absent, many sons will remain in Lo-Debar. It is our heavenly Father's desire to connect spiritual fathers to their sons. He knows how to give us what we need. He knows how to get us out of Lo-Debar.

LAVISH RESTORATION

A portion of Partnership International's work in Africa has centered on building homes for select families who are living in extreme poverty. This work began years ago on an exploratory trip when our team met a man named Rudy. He and his family lived in a small mud hut in a village we now work with regularly. Our small exploration party was walking through the village, and we noticed a dejected-looking man sitting with his head down in front of a very meager structure where he and his family lived. I could not understand his language, but his demeanor was so lowly that it broke us. As we learned his story, we discovered that he wanted to work but could find no opportunities. He reluctantly let us tour his family's mud hut. I estimate that the entire family had fewer than twenty-five possessions, including their articles of clothing. To say that they were poor is an understatement.

Rudy was a humiliated man because he could not take care of his family. He was truly living in a form of Lo-Debar, as no one could or would help him. He was forgotten, and it seemed like he was out of moves. There were hundreds of families we could have helped that day, but Rudy caught my heart and the hearts of the leaders who were with me. We pooled resources and hired a few local men to help us. By the end of the week, we had built Rudy a new two-bedroom home and filled it with furniture. The family was so grateful for their new home, and this initial project sparked a movement that was responsible for the construction of dozens more rescue homes in the impoverished village.

What struck me most about this first house project was Rudy's transformation. We have visited him many times and showcased his house as an example of the "first one." No longer dejected, Rudy stands tall with confidence, and his family is doing much better. His story is celebrated in his village, and he has become a catalyst of generosity. Many more families have been helped because of the vision that began with Rudy. He still faces many challenges, but he no longer lives in Lo-Debar.

Mephibosheth's story could have turned out very differently than it did. If not for the grace of King David, he probably would have been completely forgotten or even killed. He easily could have lived out his days in obscurity. Remaining hidden was really his best defense against a shameful lineage he never asked for. But, in His loving providence, God always has a better plan for His sons. Our Father's graceful intention is one of salvation and restoration—not insignificance followed by destruction. Mephibosheth would not be forgotten. He would be remembered and restored in the most lavish way.

> *When he came to David, he bowed low to the ground in deep respect. David said, "Greetings, Mephibosheth." Mephibosheth replied, "I am your servant." "Don't be afraid!" David said. "I intend to show kindness to you because of my promise to your father, Jonathan."*
> (2 Samuel 9:6–7)

Mephibosheth approached David with fear and respect. He probably thought his number was up. He had been found, and even if he could run, there was no place to go. King David wasted no time in announcing his kind intentions and reciting his covenant with his friend Jonathan. Mephibosheth must have felt such surprise and relief. I imagine that just to be speaking with the king was healing in itself.

I love that David specifically mentioned Jonathan. The death of David's friend occurred when Mephibosheth was only five years old. He had heard of his father's exploits, but he had had little time to truly know him. Mephibosheth lived on the few memories and fading images of a father he barely knew. David stood in Jonathan's place, honoring their covenant even after Jonathan's death. This covenantal blessing saved Mephibosheth. This is classic spiritual fatherhood, and King David made it look easy. What a powerful picture it is.

Whether you are a biological or spiritual dad, it is your responsibility to speak to the future of your sons and daughters.

If it weren't for the covenant made between Jonathan and David, Mephibosheth would not have been saved. His future depended on the words of his father—words spoken many years earlier. This is another "type" illustrating the fact that our God is a covenant-keeping God! *"God...is the faithful God who keeps his covenant for a thousand generations"* (Deuteronomy 7:9). God's own "father heart" is to honor the blessings and agreements we make with Him concerning our children. We must pray and prophesy over their lives. Someday, one of your own kids may be in Lo-Debar in need of rescue.

ROYAL TABLES

One of the more powerful autobiographies that was adapted as a movie is the story of Antwone Fisher. The book is a memoir called *Finding Fish,* and the 2002 film directed and starring Denzel Washington was called *Antwone Fisher.* It is the true story of an abused young man who is trying to find his path in life. Antwone's father was killed before Antwone was born, and his teenage mother was put in jail. He was placed in an orphanage but ultimately ended up in an abusive foster home, where he was physically and emotionally mistreated and even molested. Antwone ended up a homeless teenager until he decided to join the navy to turn his life around. There, he met Dr. Jerome Davenport, who would be both his therapist and a kind of father to him.

Finding Fish is told in chronological order, but the film relies on flashbacks to relay Antwone's story. In the movie, there are two beautiful dinner scenes. The first, near the beginning of the film, is an imaginative dream; the second, near the end of the film, is a depiction of something that really happened.

In the first dinner scene, Antwone is welcomed as a boy into a large barn where a massive Thanksgiving-style dinner has been prepared. He walks past generations of his family, who are all happy that he is there. He then is seated at the head of the table, only to wake up before the feast begins.

The second dinner scene is the powerful climax of the film. Antwone confronts his abusers and reunites with his aunt, who invites him to meet his real family. Just as in the dream, he is greeted by generations as he walks into his aunt's home. Then, double doors are opened to reveal a massive banquet table filled with delicious food. At the end of the table are the older generations of his family, and an elderly grandmother is in the head seat. She grasps Antwone's face in both her hands and, with passion, says, "Welcome." Then, the feast begins. The inference is powerful. Antwone is welcomed to a table that was his all along. He is rightfully restored.

There are many similarities between Antwone's story and that of Mephibosheth. Both individuals faced isolation and pain due to their family's decisions. The greater correlation is in their disconnection from the rights of their family. Mephibosheth had been robbed of his place in his family lineage. His very destiny was taken from him because of choices that he was too young to have a say in. Like Antwone, Mephibosheth had missed a lifetime of family meals and celebrations. He lost his seat at the table. But that all changed the day King David invited him back to the kingdom.

David wasted little time restoring Mephibosheth, telling him, "*I will give you all the property that once belonged to your grandfather Saul, and you will eat here with me at the king's table!*" (2 Samuel 9:7). This was not a onetime occurrence; "*from that time on, Mephibosheth ate regularly at David's table, like one of the king's own sons*" (2 Samuel 9:11). David began with economic restitution by giving Mephibosheth all the land owned by his wealthy grandfather, King Saul. David then restored his position by offering Mephibosheth a seat at the table next to his own sons. This was an exclusively royal privilege, one of the greatest honors anyone could have received. His own family may have been gone, but Mephibosheth was adopted into the king's family. David had a new son.

This broken young man was moved from barrenness to a place of abundance. He was taken from a position of humiliation to a seat of honor in a matter of moments. This is, of course, what our God has done for each and every one of us. Like David, our God is intentional with the restoration of His sons. Ephesians 1:5 says, "*God decided in advance to adopt us into his own family by bringing us to himself through Jesus Christ. This is what he wanted to do, and it gave him great pleasure.*" Nothing pleases our heavenly Father more than adopting us into His family.

In Romans 8, Paul explains our "adoption" even further. You can feel his father heart as he writes: "*You have not received a spirit that makes you fearful slaves. Instead, you received God's Spirit when he adopted you as his own children. Now we call him, 'Abba, Father.' For his Spirit joins with our spirit to affirm that we are God's children. And since we are his children, we are his heirs*" (Romans 8:15–17). So, God's Spirit moves us from fear to heir. We get to move from the slavery of our fearful existence to inheriting the very kingdom of God! This is Mephibosheth's story, and it is ours too. We are sons of God.

I want you to see two more aspects of what David did for Mephibosheth (and what God does for us). First, let's look at his placement at the table. I love the fact that when Mephibosheth sat at the table with David's other sons, his condition was covered by his position. The table itself would have shielded the view of Mephibosheth's injuries. When he sat at the king's table, there was an equality there that he could not have gotten anywhere else. God's grace covers our limitations.

At the king's table resided the good looks and boundless ambition of Absalom, the strength and courage of Joab, the brilliance of Solomon, and the boundless confidence of David's many advisers. Now, at that same table, sat a broken young man from a forgotten place with wounds who could no longer speak for him. Mephibosheth was given a voice, a place, and a royal seat at the king's table.

Second, let's talk about the food. Can you imagine what an upgrade in diet this must have been for Mephibosheth? But that is not why the food mattered so much. There is something deeper going on here. Out of all the things David could have said to relay his desire to bless Mephibosheth, he chose to talk about the king's table. He chose to invite him to regularly share royal meals with his own sons.

Food is a huge deal in the Bible. We know that Israel had several significant rituals centered around a meal. We know that when Jesus ate with sinners, it made the religious people angry. (See Matthew 9:10–17.) In fact, arguments about who should eat with whom are found all throughout the New Testament. In our culture, we may not be all that particular about the people with whom we eat, but the people in the Bible sure were.

In their culture, eating with someone was a sign of acceptance. This is why Jesus eating with sinners and the apostles eating with Gentiles made such a stir. Mephibosheth's being invited to the king's table is yet another metaphor that speaks to the way God loves us. Every bite of every meal at the king's table was a testament to the fact that he was loved and no longer forgotten.

Probably my favorite "food moment" in the Bible is found near the end of John's gospel. In John 21, we are told seven disciples went fishing. They all abandoned Jesus when He was being crucified, and now it seemed that they were going back to their former profession. Then, they saw a man standing on the shore. He called out to them and told them to drop their nets on the other side of the boat. They obeyed, and suddenly, they were catching so many fish that the net couldn't handle it. They knew it was Jesus.

Peter, the one who denied Christ three times before His crucifixion, was the first to jump in the water and swim ashore. The other six followed with the boat, and within minutes, seven soggy former disciples stood before Jesus. Every last one of them had abandoned Jesus when He needed them the most. Now, they were standing before Him after He had conquered death itself. I can only imagine the humiliation and shame they must have been feeling.

Then Jesus did an act of restorative grace that each of them would have fully recognized. He got some bread and fish that He had been preparing on the beach, and He fed them. He shared a meal with them even though they had failed Him. None of the disciples would have even dared to ask Him who He was. (See John 21:12.) They didn't speak, they just ate. The first thing a resurrected Jesus chose to do was to feed His spiritual sons.

There are extravagant tables like this available to you and me. We must partake because we cannot invite others to the table of grace unless we have dined there ourselves. Practically speaking, this would be a great strategy for any aspiring spiritual father to adopt. Maybe set up that men's breakfast you have been thinking about starting at your church. Be the catalyst of a wild game supper where men can tell stories of the hunt. Or just invite some men to your home, where you can show off your skills with the grill. Food has a way of opening people up. The invitation to share a meal together still has astounding relational power. Even today, the tables of spiritual fathers and sons are where royal things happen.

GENERATIONAL GENEROSITY

It is important to note that the generosity shown here by David is touching generations. Second Samuel 9:12 tells us that Mephibosheth had a young son named Micah. This royal great-grandson of King Saul only gets marginal references in Scripture. (See 1 Chronicles 8:34.) Mephibosheth's restoration meant that his own son could receive the benefit of his father's royalty. David's kindness would surpass Mephibosheth's immediate existence. This is the kind of impact that is attached to the liberality of spiritual fathers. When you invest in a spiritual son or daughter, you are touching every generation that will come from them. Your work in the present transcends time.

The word *transcend* relates to an attribute of God. Our God is transcendent. This is a big theological concept that simply means God is beyond time and space. He is wholly independent from the physical and chronological limitations of this universe. Psalm 119:90 (NIV) tells us that God's "*faithfulness continues through all generations*"; He "*established the earth, and it endures.*" *The Message* translation says, "*I see the limits to everything human, but the horizons can't contain your commands!*" (Psalm 119:96 MSG). When you obey God and invest in others, you are working beyond human limitations. The work we do with our spiritual sons and daughters crosses over time and space.

One of the false challenges of reaching young people is what I call "the lie of relevance." This is when we fall into the trap of thinking we have to be cooler than we are to reach someone from a different generation. The truth is that we have something far greater than relevance. We have transcendence! The testimony of what God can do will never grow old. Every generation needs spiritual fathers and even spiritual grandfathers. This is an inherent need that refuses to go out of style. Stop trying to relate and just be a father. Stop trying to be cool and just become a son.

A few years ago, I joyously held my grandson for the first time. As soon as he was placed in my arms, I could feel the providence of God in his life. God spoke profoundly to my spirit about his calling, and I am still in the process of understanding it. Someday, I will have a God-ordained conversation with him about his future. I couldn't help but feel the immediate weight of another generation being placed on my shoulders—I knew I could not let him down. I cherish being a grandfather, and my bond with my grandsons is growing stronger. The key is not growing inward as you grow older; my age is an asset, and so is yours. More experience, wisdom, and discernment means you have more to give to younger generations.

In the upcoming relationships we will explore together, you will see that Israel becomes a more complicated kingdom to rule. Just like David's graceful actions are crossing time, so are the evil actions of Saul. Second Samuel 21 is one of those moments. Years after the death of Saul, the Gibeonites came to King David demanding justice for Saul's attacks on their relatives. David needed alliances at the time because of the division

WHEN YOU INVEST IN A SPIRITUAL SON OR DAUGHTER, YOU ARE TOUCHING EVERY GENERATION THAT WILL COME FROM THEM. YOUR WORK IN THE PRESENT TRANSCENDS TIME.

in his kingdom caused by his son Absalom. He agreed to let the rest of Saul's sons be handed over to them, but *"the king spared Jonathan's son Mephibosheth, who was Saul's grandson, because of the oath David and Jonathan had sworn before the LORD"* (2 Samuel 21:7).

Once again, we see the "fatherly covenant" Jonathan made with David reaching out from the grave to save his son. If it had not been for the voice of his father, Mephibosheth would have been killed by the others. I cannot stress this enough: fathers possess the power of generational generosity. It is worth the time and the struggle to speak into the future of someone who may be decades behind you. You are never more like God than when spiritually invested in the life of a "Mephibosheth." God will always honor the work of fathers toward their sons. After all, this is what He has trained us to do. He is the perfect Father.

SPECIAL CALLING

Let me address one last thing before I close this chapter. Sometimes, I hear the concept of spiritual fatherhood being attacked by "online theologians" or people who have been hurt by an abusive leader. Now, we can all attest that any relationship with someone in authority has the potential to bring harm if that authority is misused. But let's not deny the biblical foundation for what we are studying. We have dozens of biblical examples, but we also have the direct words of Scripture from the apostle Paul.

> *Even if you had ten thousand guardians in Christ, you do not have many fathers, for in Christ Jesus I became your father through the gospel."* (1 Corinthians 4:15 NIV)

Paul clearly believed that there was a special calling for him to be a father to the Corinthian church. It is a unique role that does not come along every day. Most of us will not "father" an entire church by being the first one to introduce them to the gospel. But we all can be a father to someone, and we all can submit ourselves to the role of being a son. Let us not allow our imperfect experiences to rob us of this perfect gift.

Many will teach you something, but a few will go deeper, and a few will be a father to you. A few will help you find your way out of your Lo-Debar. So, set your personal radar toward the discovery of spiritual sons and fathers. God is not looking for experts on the subject. He just needs a few willing men who will submit to this call to rescue and be rescued.

7

POWERFUL PROPHETS (DAVID & NATHAN)

> *Then Nathan said to David, "You are that man!"*
> —2 Samuel 12:7

Two decades ago, I led one of my first large mission teams on a trip to Ecuador. We were partnering with another amazing organization called OneHope, and their president, a fantastic man named Rob, was also there. Rob was hosting donors and had a hectic speaking schedule. One afternoon, I received a call from Rob's assistant, who informed me that Rob had taken an emergency flight out because he was very sick. They asked me to take over Rob's speaking schedule, and I happily agreed. It turned out that he was suffering from a case of altitude sickness. Quito, Ecuador, is over 9,000 feet above sea level, and it was affecting him so severely that it posed a threat to his very life. Rob had to descend to a lower altitude, or the consequences would be dire.

A combination of lower air pressure and reduced oxygen levels is what causes altitude sickness. The dangers can increase depending on how quickly someone ascends to a higher altitude. The symptoms can be extreme: dizziness, fatigue, nausea, vision changes, and rapid heart rate. Ascending to high mountaintops comes with dangers that you will never know in the valley.

King David experienced the spiritual equivalent of this phenomenon in 2 Samuel 11–12. Decades before the events recorded in these chapters, David faced Goliath in a place called the Valley of Elah. In that lowly place, there was an abundance of "spiritual oxygen" to breathe. Now David had reached the highest heights as king, and the air had become thin. He was now in a palace on the mountaintop of all his achievements, and he could hardly breathe. There were no giants to fight here or mad kings to run from. His faith and courage were barely needed anymore.

In 2 Samuel 11, David's pride was sucking the spiritual life right out of his royal lungs. He was no longer a lowly shepherd. No longer restricted by the walls of a cave or his impossible dreams. He was the rightfully established king and wielded more power than most men could even dream of. When you get to this part of David's story, it is as if the adventure novel has turned into a horror story. David's behavior had become barely recognizable. He was not pursuing his calling, and he certainly was not pursuing God. God is not mentioned until verse 27 of chapter 11. David was experiencing spiritual altitude sickness, and he was in grave danger.

CATASTROPHIC ARROGANCE

Second Samuel 11 opens with King David in an unfamiliar position. Verse 1 says, *"When kings normally go out to war, David...stayed behind in Jerusalem."* Theologians estimate that David was in his fifties when he stayed behind at the palace that day. David's spiritual altitude sickness is displayed in his confusion, blindness, pride, arrogance, and lack of wisdom. To make matters worse, he was unaware of the severity of his illness. Pride has a way of blinding us to what is really happening. Pride dwells on the mountaintops of our lives and always seeks to push us off a cliff. Wisdom is rarely found in high places. This is why even kings need to visit valleys regularly.

Pride goes before destruction, and haughtiness before a fall.
(Proverbs 16:18)

When pride comes, then comes disgrace, but with humility comes wisdom. (Proverbs 11:2 NIV)

David's pride is evident in how he abused his power. He used his position as king repeatedly to commit this sin. Let's count the ways: In 2 Samuel 11:1, David shirked his responsibilities and sent Joab to fight alongside the Israelite army. Then, after viewing Bathsheba from his palace roof, David has a servant inquire about her. David summoned her by way of messengers; she arrived at the palace, and they committed adultery. (See 2 Samuel 11:3–4.) David's lack of shame in his behavior is shocking.

After sleeping with Bathsheba, David commanded Joab to have Uriah, Bathsheba's husband, return to Jerusalem from war. He even attempted to manipulate Uriah by sending him home to sleep with Bathsheba and cover up her pregnancy.

PRIDE HAS A WAY OF BLINDING US TO WHAT IS REALLY HAPPENING. PRIDE DWELLS ON THE MOUNTAINTOPS OF OUR LIVES AND ALWAYS SEEKS TO PUSH US OFF A CLIFF.

(See 2 Samuel 11:6, 8.) David's plan failed because of Uriah's integrity, so he used his kingly authority to commit murder, sending orders for Uriah to be sent into the fiercest battle so he would surely be killed. (See 2 Samuel 11:9–21.) After Uriah was killed and Bathsheba mourned her husband, she became one of David's wives. (See 2 Samuel 11:27.) All of this happened because of David's efforts to cover up his sin.

Every last one of these sinful moves required the involvement and abuse of others. You know you've taken sinning to another level when you involve others to help you do it. David did that in spades—he crossed too many lines to count. His sin of lust was fueled by an evil abuse of power.

David's actions in 2 Samuel 11 are a cautionary tale. He was a man who had unlimited power and opportunity, and his successes presented him with occasions for extreme good or evil. He failed his entire kingdom by exhibiting laziness, pridefulness, abusiveness, selfishness, and lustfulness. He failed God. Be careful what you wish for. Mountaintop dwellers face temptations that those in the valley have never seen.

I remember when news of golfer Tiger Woods's infidelity was reported everywhere. He lost his marriage, harmed his family, and so much more. He was judged by millions, including people in the church. During this time, I mentored a group of men, and I found myself correcting them about their judgmental attitudes toward Woods. Most of us would destroy ourselves if we lived at the heights that some men live. We can't imagine the pressure David faced and the temptations that came alongside the opportunities. We will not excuse his actions, but maybe we can have some empathy. If it were not for God's grace, any of us could fall in the worst way. We all are prone to the sickness that pride creates.

SILENT SEASON

David traveled so deep into the territory of sin that he could no longer find his way out. There is a season of silence between the last verse of 2 Samuel 11 and the first verse of chapter 12. We have no record of confession or genuine repentance. We know from a couple of psalms attached to this story that this was a time of misery for King David. He had become a composer without a song in his heart, a warrior with no battle to fight, a worshipper who had offended the God he worshipped. These were not blissful days for the newlywed. These were days of misery as David found himself far from the heart of God.

After his repentance, David would write about languishing in his sin, lamenting: *"When I refused to confess my sin, my body wasted away, and I groaned all day long. Day and night your hand of discipline was heavy on me. My strength evaporated like water in the summer heat"* (Psalm 32:3–4). In Psalm 51, his psalm of repentance, David acknowledges that this was a season where his sin haunted him. (See verse 3.) He was joyless, *"broken,"* and filled with *"guilt"* (verses 8–9). He was without a sense of God's presence. (See verse 11.) He had lost his ability to lead. (See verse 18.) David was in agony and needed help. He needed a voice greater than his own. The king needed someone to break the silence.

UNWANTED GIFTS

Have you ever received a gift you needed but didn't want? Maybe a pack of tube socks on Christmas morning or a gym membership for your birthday "present"? Hopefully, you are not one of the husbands who bought your wife the vacuum of her dreams for your last anniversary. I advise you never to buy anything with a cord attached to it for your wife or girlfriend—it never ends well! I came across a story recently about a man whose wife had been having dreams in which she received a gift of expensive jewelry. The man told his wife that if she would be patient, she would find out the meaning of her dreams on Valentine's Day. When the big day arrived, she opened her gift with great anticipation, only to find that her husband had bought her a book entitled *The Meaning of Dreams*. I bet that did not end well for him at all. We can do better!

The truth is, sometimes the gift we need is not the gift we want. I am so grateful that God has a habit of sending the perfect gifts at the right time. A big part of our maturing process is the merging of wants and needs. The older I get, the more I think a good pair of socks would be an excellent gift. This maturation process is also spiritual. The closer I get to Jesus, the more I want what He wants. The more I seek Him, the more He gives me the very *"desires of [my] heart"* (Psalm 37:4 NIV). Wanting the right things comes from an ever-increasing desire to know Him more.

King David was so spiritually off-center in this tragic moment that he did not know what he needed. His self-inflicted wounds were bleeding everywhere he went. He was hurting, and he had no real remedy. His very actions tell us that he wanted to move on without dealing with the consequences of what he had done. He wanted to regain the favor of God, but he also wanted his sin to remain hidden. David was desiring "gifts" that do not exist in the economy of God. He was asking God to skip over His principles, and God wouldn't do that—not even for David. So, in His great grace, God did not send David the escape he was hoping for. Instead, He sent him what he needed. He sent him a mighty prophet named Nathan.

We first see Nathan come on the scene in 2 Samuel 7. David had settled into the palace, and God had given him a measure of rest from his enemies. So, the king began thinking about the ark of God. The ark was a representation of the very presence of God. David loved God's presence so much that he wanted the ark to be close to him. This would be no easy task because the ark was so holy; to handle it, you had to know what you were doing. So King David called on a well-known man of God named Nathan, a prophet who was qualified to advise the king. Nathan told David, "*Go ahead and do whatever you have in mind, for the* L{\scriptsize ORD} *is with you*" (2 Samuel 7:3). This would be the first of many times Nathan would help David, but never was his role more important than in 2 Samuel 12.

Can you imagine how Nathan must have felt when God spoke to him about the king's sin? It must have grieved him and terrified him at the same time. Second Samuel 12:1 says, "*So the* L{\scriptsize ORD} *sent Nathan the prophet.*" This was a dangerous assignment for Nathan. He was confronting a king who was actively covering up his sin. David could have had him punished or killed. Nathan truly deserved a medal for taking on this task. Thank God that He loves us enough to send a convicting voice when we are lost in our sins. Everyone needs a Nathan from time to time.

I believe David was ready to be confronted—even if he would not admit it. He had been miserable for months. That misery had softened his heart, and he needed to get right with God. You cannot help someone who is still flexing their pride. Prodigal sons do not get saved on their way to the "far-off country" with a pocket of money. Only in the pigpen of their regret can they be reached. (See Luke 15:11–32.) David was standing in his mess. He needed someone to help him see it. He needed the power of a prophet.

Nathan began his confrontation with a God-given story. He told David about a rich man who abused his power. This wealthy man owned many sheep and cattle, yet he stole a little lamb belonging to his poor neighbor. He killed the poor man's lamb and fed it to his dinner guests. (See 2 Samuel 12:1–4.) David was so furious that he vowed to intervene and seek justice in the situation. He wanted to kill the rich man and pay back the poor man four times over. (See verses 5–6.) Nathan said to David, *"You are that man!"* (2 Samuel 12:7). Four words and David was pulled from the shadows into the light. The king was exposed. This was like a doctor placing his lamp above a wound, allowing surgery to begin. David's healing could finally start.

Nathan explained the similarities between the story and David's sin, then pronounced God's judgment. Through Nathan, God told David, *"You did it secretly, but I will make this happen to you openly in the sight of all Israel"* (2 Samuel 12:12). David was torn asunder. It had to be painful—but it also had to be a relief. There will be consequences. No one can escape the consequences of the harvest that follows when one deliberately chooses to sin. At least David's future would be lived in the light. The prophet spoke, and the king didn't have to hide anymore.

CLEANSING CONFESSION

In December 2003, Operation Red Dawn had its biggest win of the Iraq War. Around half past eight in the evening, local time, Saddam Hussein was found huddled in a "spider hole" near a farmhouse close to his hometown of Tikrit, Iraq. The operation was executed by Joint Operations Task Force 121, an elite special operations team. Hussein did not resist capture, but finding him was no easy task. One hundred fifty thousand soldiers were looking for him—yet a farmer hid the dictator for

235 days. The images of his capture would be on our screens within hours. This event triggered the first period of calmness in the war. It raised optimism in the ranks and marked the total defeat of Hussein's evil reign.[16]

I have met many men who have crawled into their own emotional and spiritual "spider holes." They do this by refusing to let anyone into their private worlds. Their sin may not be as serious as that of an evil dictator but is no less real. So, they crawl into a hiding place where anything personal is off-limits, and shameful things are buried where no one can ever find them. Their captivity is a form of torture, and their greatest fear is that someone will find out who they are. This is the type of prison in which David had put himself. On the outside, it may have looked like a luxury palace, but the king within was a prisoner. The only way out of this type of bondage is through confession, which is precisely what David did. He told Nathan everything. He came out of his hiding place.

Second Samuel 12:13 says, "*Then David confessed to Nathan, 'I have sinned against the* Lord.'" The words David had feared saying flowed across his lips and found their way into the prophet's ears. A great weight was lifted. Psalm 32:5 describes what David felt at that moment:

> *Then I let it all out; I said, "I'll come clean about my failures to* God." *Suddenly the pressure was gone—my guilt dissolved, my sin disappeared.*   (Psalm 32:5 msg)

---

16. DIA Public Affairs, "Our Place in History: 'We Got Him!' The Anniversary of the Capture of Saddam Hussein," Defense Intelligence Agency, December 13, 2013, https://www.dia.mil/News-Features/Articles/Article-View/Article/566928/our-place-in-history-we-got-him-the-anniversary-of-the-capture-of-saddam-hussein/.

Relief is not a strong enough word to describe what David was experiencing. He threw himself at the court's mercy, even if it cost him his kingdom and his life—at least he would be free.

Nathan replied, *"Yes, but the LORD has forgiven you, and you won't die for this sin"* (2 Samuel 12:13). David was forgiven, and God declared through Nathan that his life would be spared. There would still be consequences, some of which would be great—but David's life could begin again. He deeply and fully repented and was led to a place of freedom by the obedience of a brave prophet. Verse 15 tells us that Nathan returned home after the confrontation. Nathan continued to be involved with David's kingdom throughout his life, but this was his most significant contribution. He helped rescue the king.

This same opportunity for freedom is available to us. The power of confession is not just for backslidden preachers or fallen political leaders. Nothing is more courageous than a willingness to confess our sins.

> *Confess your sins to each other and pray for each other so that you may be healed. The earnest prayer of a righteous person has great power and produces wonderful results.*
>
> (James 5:16)

James commands two actions and gives two promises. We are to confess and pray. If we do, we can expect healing and wonderful results. We often quote the part about *"the earnest prayer of a righteous person"* being powerful and effective without mentioning the part about confession. James is saying that nothing moves the hand of God like the practice of transparency in our relationships. Confession opens new realms for those who are brave enough to practice it.

NOTHING IS MORE COURAGEOUS
THAN A WILLINGNESS TO
CONFESS OUR SINS.

This is part of the reason I am such an encourager of small groups of men meeting with each other. One way to experience the power of a brave prophet is to invite the wisdom of other men into your imperfect, private world. You must use wisdom and keep your circle small—but you need to have men in your life so you can admit your weaknesses. This is one of the best ways to break the hold of addictions. When a behavior grips you so tightly that you can't escape, it must be brought into the open to defeat it. Addiction thrives in the dark and hates the light. Confession is an authentic step toward living in the light and moving away from the darkness.

BECOMING DANGEROUS

> Before my father died, he said the worst thing about growing old was that other men stopped seeing you as dangerous. I've always remembered that, how being dangerous was sacred, a badge of honor. You live your life by a code, an ethos. Every man does. It's your shoreline. It's what guides you home. —Lieutenant Rorke Denver, *Act of Valor*[17]

You are not called to safety. God did not create you to be safe. He created you to be dangerous. One of the great tragedies of David's fall is that he chose his bed over his battle. He chose the safety of a palace over the risk of the battlefield. This choice helped the enemy deliver his greatest blow. King David did not fall while he was in the fray of his calling, wearing armor and carrying a sword. It was while he was wearing a silk robe on a roof with his guard down that the enemy found his access. While David was dangerous, it seemed that nothing could

---

17. Quotes, *Act of Valor*, "Dave: Chief Dave," IMDb.com, https://www.imdb.com/title/tt1591479/characters/nm4917569.

touch him. It was only when he skipped his battle that the king became vulnerable.

A moment at the beginning of the movie *Rocky III* speaks to what I am talking about. You are probably familiar with the *Rocky* movies. The scene I'm talking about is when Rocky is confronted by a character named Clubber Lang. He is a fierce boxer who wants to fight Rocky and keeps taunting and challenging him. But the champ's trainer, Mickey, won't let it happen. After several altercations with Lang, Rocky tries to force Mickey to book the fight. Finally, the fighter and trainer have it out in the upstairs bedroom of his mansion. Among the trappings of all his success, Rocky begs Mickey to let him in the ring with Clubber. Mickey refuses and even threatens to quit.

Mickey turns to Rocky and says, "Three years ago you was supernatural. You was hard and you was nasty and you had this cast-iron jaw but then the worst thing happened to you, that could happen to any fighter. You got civilized."[18] He then encourages Rocky to retire. The champ refuses, and against his better judgment, Mickey books the fight. Rocky gets destroyed. Comfort had stolen Rocky's ability to conquer. Champions are not created or maintained in comfort. Struggle is essential for warriors. When you take away conflict, men become less than dangerous. This is exactly what happened to David—he became civilized. It could happen to any of us.

After Nathan departed from David, the Bible says that God sent a sickness to the child conceived by Bathsheba. (See 2 Samuel 12:15.) David pleaded with God, but, seven days later, the child died. (See verse 18.) David comforted his wife, and she soon became pregnant again. The child she would birth would

---

18. Quotes, *Rocky III*, "Burgess Meredith: Mickey Goldmill," IMDb.com, https://www.imdb.com/title/tt0084602/characters/nm0580565.

be the future King Solomon. That is a redemption story—an example of God's amazing mercy. David had been through the wringer because of his sin. His life has been upended, and there was more struggle to come. But it is time for him to get back into the fight.

By my estimation, David had not led his army or been in battle for nearly two years. During this entire time, the battles of Israel were being fought by his commander, Joab, and a portion of his army. Now, they were about to defeat a city called Rabbah, and David was summoned by some messengers who told him that the men needed their king. (See 2 Samuel 12:26–28.) The people of Israel needed to see David back in battle. They need him to be a warrior again. *"So David gathered the rest of the army and went to Rabbah, and he fought against it and captured it"* (2 Samuel 12:29). He led his army as God had destined him to do. David was becoming dangerous again.

A brave prophet's role is to call men back to their assigned wars. Prophets correct us but also move us away from the pacifism and passivity that sin creates. Sin diminishes our strength and undermines our mindset until we are entirely out of the fight. We all need to take time for repentance and healing after we fall, but that season should be temporary. David's going to Rabbah was the first sign that the king was back in the fight.

I believe that Scripture reveals a symbolic meaning after David's victory at Rabbah. *"David removed the crown from the king's head, and it was placed on his own head. The crown was made of gold and set with gems, and it weighed seventy–five pounds"* (2 Samuel 12:30). David tried on the seventy-five-pound crown of the king he had just defeated! This was a clear indication that his royal calling was reawakening within him. He was remembering what it meant to be king. The heaviness of the crown reminded David of the weight of responsibility God assigned him to carry. God chose David to remain king, and he was preparing his mind to lead.

God has incredible plans for you, each with its dangers. A safe life is not the promise of Jesus (see John 16:33), but a significant life is. God's will has taken me to many dangerous places. He has protected me and urged me to run to the front lines where the fiercest action exists. My friend Mark Batterson, author of *All In*, writes, "Jesus did not die to make us safe. He died to make us dangerous. Faithfulness is not holding the fort. It is storming the gates of hell. The will of God is not an insurance plan. It is a daring plan."[19] It's time to get back to the battle—you are needed there.

RADICAL ROUTINES

The most significant catalyst for David's failure in 2 Samuel 11 may have been the unhealthy change in his routine. We know he *"stayed behind"* instead of going to war, leading to temptation he didn't flee. (See 2 Samuel 11:1.) *"One evening David got up from his bed and walked around on the roof of his palace. From the roof he saw a woman bathing. The woman was very beautiful"* (2 Samuel 11:2 NIV). David was just getting out of bed, and it was evening already. Some versions say he was awake from a nap, but most translations do not specify. We know that he was sleeping when he should have been off fighting. The king had developed a horrible routine.

His weak routine set up the strong temptation he faced that day. The man who was usually disciplined had become a creature of impulse. His new routine would lead him to a reality he

---

19. Mark Batterson, *All In: You Are One Decision Away from a Totally Different Life* (Grand Rapids, MI: Zondervan, 2013), 13–14.

never imagined. A few "off" days or weeks led him to years of residual consequences. The funny thing is, the ramifications of our routines are without prejudice. They will produce a harvest in our lives for our good or our destruction. Your routine will ruin or rescue you. The repetitions you foster will either fulfill your destiny or rob you of it.

One of the reasons we need brave prophets in our lives is to call us out on our poor routines. They have the spiritual vision to see down the road and warn us of the disaster we are heading toward. They can also call us to greater routines that produce a greater harvest of success and impact for the kingdom. Prophets move us toward radical routines.

When I started writing this book, my temptation was to clear my calendar of all meetings—especially the many mentoring calls on my schedule. The Holy Spirit urged me to keep them on my calendar, and He assured me that He would make up the time. So, I canceled no calls. Instead, I used my meetings to mentor men in a more radical way. I used my writing routine to call men to a higher level.

One of the analogies I have been using in my conversations is the condition of my front yard. We have very sandy soil in which grass has a difficult time growing. A sprinkler system is a must where we live, but our system lacked sprayers near the edge of our yard. This lack of coverage resulted in the grass around the edges of our yard dying every year. To rectify the problem, we installed additional sprinkler heads. We had to pay attention to the edges.

I find that most people take care of the center of their lives. They must show up to work to collect a paycheck. They must be faithful to the basics, or everything will fall apart. But they

ONE OF THE REASONS WE NEED BRAVE PROPHETS IN OUR LIVES IS TO CALL US OUT ON OUR POOR ROUTINES. THEY HAVE THE SPIRITUAL VISION TO SEE DOWN THE ROAD AND WARN US OF THE DISASTER WE ARE HEADING TOWARD.

tend to neglect the edges. The "edges" of our lives and callings are the places where extra discipline is required. The edges are where things like that book you have wanted to write live. The edges are where you will find the time to start that Bible study and mentor other men. The edges are where you must live if you will ever find the time and money to go on that mission trip. The edges are where treasure is buried, but you need a better routine to uncover it. Prophets guide us to the edges.

The question of the hour for all men today is, "What aspects of your life currently do not deserve a place in your routine?" My golf score may never break eighty because the practice required by that sport is not worthy of my routine. I may never kill that world-record buck or catch that ten-pound bass I have been after. I probably won't catch up on all the TV shows I have meant to watch. My radical routines have only so much room for frivolous pursuits. In Psalm 119:37, the psalmist writes, *"Turn my eyes from worthless things."* That is my prayer for you. May the patterns of your life line up with the purpose God has for you. May your routines be worthy of your calling.

PROPHETIC PROTECTION

This part of David's life could have read much differently if Nathan had been injected into it sooner. What if David had asked him to visit at the beginning of his ill-planned vacation? What if the king had permitted Nathan to come into his life regularly? What if the man after God's own heart had opened his heart to a corrective voice sooner? David could have avoided a world of pain. Prophets are given to us for our protection. They are gifts from God, but we must be willing to receive them.

I believe your heart is more open than most if you have read this chapter. So, let me give you some closing advice: First, prophets are sent; they are not found. Most of us already have a person in mind who has unique, God-given insight into our lives. Second, prophets need an open invitation. Someone correcting you or guiding you without your permission is an exercise in futility. Third, prophetic conversations work best when they are ongoing. When you find the right voice, you should meet with them regularly. Finally, the access of a trusted prophet should be unfettered. No one should ever be expected to help you while you close your life to them.

Most of our Davidic lessons have been from the positive side of the coin. This chapter teaches us what not to do from our beloved example. I would implore you in this rare case: don't be like David. Use your power for good and bring the right voices into the very throne room of your life. Even kings—especially kings—need a Nathan, or they will become their own worst enemy. You are never too important to acknowledge your character flaws. We all need the protection of a prophet.

8

MIGHTY MENTORS (DAVID & JOAB)

*You use steel to sharpen steel,
and one friend sharpens another.*
—Proverbs 27:17 (MSG)

I enjoy fishing in the seventeen-acre lake in our subdivision. I have a small, two-person, two-seat boat about ten feet long with pontoons on each side. I joined a few social media groups with like-minded owners of the same type of vessel. One group is called "Tiny Boat Nation," and several others exist. You wouldn't believe people's modifications and upgrades to these small boats. Most often, the men who own these vessels tend to get rid of the second boat seat. They jettison their ability to take a passenger to help with the weight of their modifications or to make room for more equipment. I decided I would never do that. Having a better-equipped ride is not nearly as important as making room for another fisherman. I decided that I didn't want to fish alone.

The problem with my commitment to inviting other men into my angling world is that most (not all) of them are not experienced fishermen. They did not grow up with a rod and reel in their hands like I did, and problems inevitably arise when I try to teach them how to fish. Lines get caught in trees. Hooks fly close to heads. I usually don't catch as many fish as usual when I have another man in the boat. But what I do catch is way more important. When you spend time in nature with someone, they tend to open up more. You catch their heart and hear their struggles. While I mentor them about casting or setting the hook, we often find ourselves diving into the deeper waters of each other's lives.

There is a clear call in Scripture to have a "second seat" available to the men we are assigned to. *"Two people are better off than one, for they can help each other succeed"* (Ecclesiastes 4:9). Jesus sent out His followers *"two by two"* (Luke 10:1 NIV) to do the work of the ministry. This flies in the face of the extreme "loner" culture we men seem to create for ourselves. The clear theme of this book is that "everyone needs someone." We actually need multiple "someone's" and different types of relationships. One of the most important ones is mentorship. Every man needs a mighty mentor.

We see several people in David's life who could qualify as mentors, but none is more significant than his complicated relationship with a man named Joab. Joab was the brother of Abishai, whom we studied in chapter five. One of the greatest warriors in the story of David, he was the commander of Israel's armies. The accounts of Joab in Scripture are fierce and wild at times, showing us both the victories and the shortcomings of this man. Many mentorship relationships are a two-way street with the one being mentored switching back and forth. This was true of the God-ordained affiliation between these two men. Joab certainly needed David, but when David lost himself in his failures and pain, Joab was the one who wore the mantle of mentorship.

We first observe this in 2 Samuel 12. As we studied in chapter seven, the king had fallen into sin and was confronted by the prophet Nathan. David stepped away from military leadership for about two years. Meanwhile, Joab was off fighting Israel's wars and was about to experience a significant victory. Joab knew that King David was the one who needed "the win" and the good publicity that would come with it. He knew David needed to get back in the fight.

> *Joab sent messengers to tell David, "I have fought against Rabbah and captured its water supply. Now bring the rest of the army and capture the city. Otherwise, I will capture it and get credit for the victory."* (2 Samuel 12:27–28)

Joab mentored the king away from his mourning and defeatism. He pulled David back into his destiny.

COMPLICATED CONDOLENCES

The next mentorship moment between Joab and David is much bigger and far more complicated. This very significant event is recorded at the beginning of 2 Samuel 19. So much happens between chapters 12 and 19, and most of it is not good. David's son Absalom gains power and attempts to take the kingdom from him, almost succeeding. At one point, the very

MANY MENTORSHIP RELATIONSHIPS ARE A TWO-WAY STREET WITH THE ONE BEING MENTORED SWITCHING BACK AND FORTH.

armies of Israel are divided and fighting one another. In a single day, 20,000 men die during the horrible civil war that Absalom causes. (See 2 Samuel 18:7.) Led by Joab, David's men prevail, but the losses are devastating. This is all due to David's wayward offspring.

The bloody conflict peaks at a strange moment when Absalom's thick hair is caught in a tree, and he dangles from it. (See 2 Samuel 18:9.) David's men fear taking Absalom's life, but Joab says, *"Enough of this nonsense"* (2 Samuel 18:14) and stabs him. Ten of Joab's men help their leader finish killing Absalom. (See 2 Samuel 18:15.) *"Then Joab blew the ram's horn, and his men returned from chasing the army of Israel"* (2 Samuel 18:16). Thousands of lives are saved, and Israel has a chance to heal and be united again. However, deep wounds remain, especially in David. The nation may have been saved, but the king has lost his son.

You cannot accurately study the life of David without the realization that you are surveying something of mammoth proportions. This is a king-sized story with royal ramifications. Raw human weakness is on display alongside divine strength. The monarchy of King David is not exempt from excruciating family drama. Much of this saga is even infected by multiple layers of evil ambition. David's story is beyond complicated.

During his worst years, David's damaged character significantly affects his leadership and judgment. This is why I believe we should have some theological grace when studying Joab's position. David's unlikely mentor is a deeply flawed character but also an important one. He stands in the middle of the consequences of David's sin and must make the most challenging choices. Somebody had to lead where David would not.

In the latter part of 2 Samuel 18, King David is in painful mourning over the death of his son Absalom.

> *The king was overcome with emotion. He went up to the room over the gateway and burst into tears. And as he went, he cried, "O my son Absalom! My son, my son Absalom! If only I had died instead of you! O Absalom, my son, my son."* (2 Samuel 18:33)

These words express the agony of loss in the broken heart of a father. David knew that his sin was partially to blame. He was filled with unimaginable grief.

David wept and mourned so much that *"all the people heard of the king's deep grief for his son"* (2 Samuel 19:2). David's grief was so unrelenting that the soldiers who fought Absalom's rebellion *"crept back into the town that day as though they were ashamed"* (verse 3). David would not stop crying, and all of Israel knew it. Understanding gave way to confusion, and even David's closest men wavered in their support. Something had to be done. Somebody needed to speak to the king.

Joab, the very person who had driven daggers into Absalom's heart, was the only one who was up to the task. In my reading of the text, I sense a willingness that is laced with conviction. Joab had to think of the bigger picture because the king was blinded by his pain. So, Joab stood in an emotionally volatile place and did what needed to be done. Joab's mentorship was not perfect, but it was providential. His kingly advice was complicated but necessary.

> *Then Joab went to the king's room and said to him, "We saved your life today and the lives of your sons, your*

daughters, and your wives and concubines. Yet you act like this, making us feel ashamed of ourselves." (2 Samuel 19:5)

Joab then told David what was evident to everyone but himself: *"You seem to love those who hate you and hate those who love you. You have made it clear today that your commanders and troops mean nothing to you. It seems that if Absalom had lived and all of us had died, you would be pleased"* (2 Samuel 19:6). David was making the worst impression, but he couldn't see it. David needed someone to awaken him from the grief that was paralyzing him.

I am sure Joab would have preferred to deliver flowers to the king instead of the truth. Everyone else was comforting, but David needed to be confronted. Mentorship is easy when you compliment a person or confirm their calling. It gets complicated when you must touch sensitive nerves that are fortified and justified by emotional trauma. This is what Joab was doing, and he did it without pulling a punch. These two men had fought side by side in countless battles. Theirs was a warrior relationship. Joab had earned his entrance into the king's court that day. Without the words of Joab, David would have lost everything.

David's commander told him that Israel's troops were hanging on by a thread and that they needed their king. He warned him that if he did not get back to leadership, the nation would fall apart entirely. Second Samuel 19:8 is a hidden gem among Bible verses that celebrate the effect of mentorship. The weight of what is happening here is monumental.

> *So the King went out and took his seat at the town gate, and as the news spread throughout the town that he was there, everyone went to him.* (2 Samuel 19:8)

David got up from his bed of mourning and became a king again. He was mentored out of the dark forest he was lost in, and although he was still hurting, he was leading again. Israel could start to heal.

The latter part of verse 8 says, *"Meanwhile, the Israelites who had supported Absalom fled to their homes."* Word spread of the king's gesture, and the people began to remember all that David had done for Israel. They said,: *"Now Absalom, whom we anointed to rule over us, is dead. Why not ask David to come back and be our king again?"* (2 Samuel 19:10). Joab had navigated a royal disaster, and he preserved David in the process. At this moment, he was the right mentor to help save a kingdom.

FLYING LESSONS

In the early days of aviation, planes were loud and often had open cockpits. If you were training someone how to fly, you would not sit next to the student as they do in modern-day planes. Instead, the experienced pilot would sit behind the trainee. To make matters more complex, the engine's noise made it impossible to hear directions. So, the instructor would tug on the back of the shirt of the pilot-in-training to communicate.

According to legend, students would cut out the back of their shirts when they graduated. Then, the cloth would be displayed in the hangar alongside those of others who had passed their training. This was a sign that they no longer needed instruction—they could now fly alone. The tradition is still practiced today by many flight schools. Hopefully, the graduates don't wear their best T-shirts on their last day![20]

Pilots with enough hours may no longer need to feel the familiar tug of instruction but will always need to be mentored. Every man at every level needs a mentor. Positions did not get more powerful than King David's, and he needed one. It was ultimately mentorship that rescued him from himself. The day you think we have graduated from the required voice of key trusted friendships is when you enter into "the danger zone" (to use a phrase from *Top Gun*!). I have decided in my own life that I will never have my "shirt cut." I crave instruction, and with the help of the Holy Spirit, I always will. Bring on the "flying lessons"—we all need them.

The key mentoring verse in all of Scripture must be Proverbs 27:17, which declares, *"As iron sharpens iron, so a friend sharpens a friend."* If you study this verse in Hebrew, you will find that the word *iron* has two different meanings. The first refers to the steel used for a knife or sword. The second references the steel used for a file or sharpening stone. You don't sharpen a knife by stroking it against another knife. Instead, you get something of a different "grain," and the contact between the two becomes abrasive and productive. You get your edge by combining similar but vastly different forces.

When it comes to mentorship, we are usually tempted to find someone similar to ourselves—maybe someone who approaches life the same way we do, or someone who is sharper than ourselves but only slightly. This would be a mistake. Mentors must be of a different "grain." They must have the courage to let sparks

---

20. "Shirt Cutting: A Tradition for First Solo Flights," *High Flight Academy*, November 6, 2018, accessed January 7, 2025, https://www.highflightacademy.com/shirt-cutting-a-tradition-for-first-solo-flights.

fly if necessary. The process can be abrasive, but that is what is required to shape us. Joab did this for David—even if the process was painful.

Another way to look at this verse is through the analogy of a blacksmith, who uses an iron hammer and anvil to shape steel into something useful. The blows make it look violent, but every strike is purposeful. The blacksmith has a vision of the potential that the object cannot see alone. Proverbs 27:6 (NIV) says, *"Wounds from a friend can be trusted."* We must "trust the process" and the intent when a mighty mentor strikes at the core of our issues, never allowing abuse, constantly testing the spirit, and never allowing any advice that contradicts Scripture to stand. This is how we become the sharp weapons we are meant to be.

The Japanese are known for crafting the finest swords in the world. To create these works of art, they have to master the process of bringing together both hard and soft steel. The blade has to be hard enough to hold an edge but soft enough not to be brittle. Some Japanese swords have over 30,000 paper-thin laminations or hard and soft steel combinations. The steel is heated, layered, folded, and pummeled repeatedly during the forging process.

Becoming a masterpiece that is also a deadly weapon is not easy. Some of the layered detail of these swords is less than a hundred thousandth of an inch thick.[21] However, the master craftsman knows what he is doing, even through all the heating, layering, folding, and pummeling. This is the level of trust God wants us to have with Him. Sometimes, God asks us to transfer

---

21. "The Secrets and Traditional Methods of Forging Japanese Swords," *Swords of Northshire*, accessed January 7, 2025, https://www.swordsofnorthshire.com/blogs/theblade/japanese-sword-forging.

that trust to mentors who can help complete the work He is doing in us.

My favorite verse translation brings out even more elements of the original language. *"Iron sharpens iron; so a man sharpens the countenance of his friend [to show rage or worthy purpose]"* (Proverbs 27:17 AMPC). Mentorship has the power to lift your countenance. It can pull you from the depths of defeat and give you the courage to return to the battle lines. If mentoring is not increasing your courage, then it is not being done correctly. If you meet with a mentor and are not filled with godly "rage" to return to your "worthy purpose," you might need a new mentor. Mentorship, by definition, should be motivational.

RELATIONAL RISK

The most remarkable aspect of Joab's mentorship with King David is the level of risk he was willing to take. Kings at that time had unlimited power. Although Joab would have been a difficult man for David to punish, it was still a distinct and extremely dangerous possibility. Mentorship is never without a level of risk.

Joab was intimately involved in the mission to preserve the Israel that David had built. He had been involved with David's mission from the very beginning. His gifts and energy had all been put on the line repeatedly for the cause. Mentors do not and should not appear out of nowhere. True mentors must be connected to your world and invested in your mission. We can dream about having that celebrity we don't know that will give us life-changing advice, but the depth of their advice will be limited. Information may be powerful, but learning from the people who are with you in your struggle is far better. Mentorship should flow out of your relationships.

WE MUST "TRUST THE PROCESS" AND THE INTENT WHEN A MIGHTY MENTOR STRIKES AT THE CORE OF OUR ISSUES, NEVER ALLOWING ABUSE, CONSTANTLY TESTING THE SPIRIT, AND NEVER ALLOWING ANY ADVICE THAT CONTRADICTS SCRIPTURE TO STAND.

We all know pastors who appear on stage and preach powerfully, only to disappear from everyone's lives until the following Sunday. Maybe you had a coach who would instruct the team and yell at the players, but he was unapproachable off the field. Or how about that absentee father who wants the privileges of fatherhood without taking the time to be a dad? Another example of this would be the military. In the armed forces, the generals are rarely mentors. The sergeants have the contact and connection to build recruits into soldiers. Mentorship happens in the trenches. If you are unwilling to get close enough to get hurt, then you will never be a real mentor.

It is important to stress again that Joab's relationship with David was tumultuous. Many of the characters in 2 Samuel led violent lives; battles, wars, killing, and death happened regularly. Joab dealt with his deep character issues and even disobeyed the king's orders. His killing of King Saul's former commander, Abner, and his cousin Amasa (see chapters 3 and 20 of 2 Samuel) are the two best examples. Sometimes, his ambition and heart for Israel were so convoluted that it's impossible to tell which one was driving him. Joab was a complex figure throughout the rest of his life, mixing helpful and hurtful actions. David would even warn the future King Solomon about Joab, and after David's death, Solomon would have him killed. (See 1 Kings 2:5–34).

Yet, despite all these sordid details, God never removed Joab from David's life or the kingdom while he was alive. Mentors are not always the people you get along with the best. Sometimes, they are the very abrasive file to your dull blade. Joab was not always the man David wanted, but he was often the man he needed.

PAINFUL PAYBACK

Occasionally, David was the one inflicting the wounds on Joab. We see this in a barely noticeable verse after Joab's big talk with David. At Joab's insistence, King David is trying to reunite Israel, but the very tribe David is from is dragging their feet. David's homeland is holding up the whole nation. Judah is the last tribe to welcome him back to the throne. Their quasi-leader was David's nephew Amasa, who had unwisely sided with Absalom's revolt. So, David, playing the politician, says to Amasa, *"Since you are my own flesh and blood, like Joab, may God strike me and even kill me if I do not appoint you as commander of my army in his place"* (2 Samuel 19:13). In other words, "Since we are related, I will go ahead and replace Joab as my commander and put you in charge." His plan works, and Amasa convinces Judah to get behind King David.

Can you imagine what that felt like for Joab? He had been risking his life for decades for the king. For the last ten years, he had led the army without much help from David. He helped David regain the kingdom, and within a short period, his position was given to someone else! It is only a tiny part of this story, and Amasa's leadership time would be brief and insincere. In fact, Amasa delays his very first assignment with the king. David orders him to bring Judah's fighting men to his needed defense, and Amasa's delay jeopardizes the kingdom. (See 2 Samuel 20:4–5.)

Joab steps in, killing Amasa, and then rallies the men to take down another uprising. Joab's actions are a mixture of self-preservation and prioritizing Israel's best interests. Was this payback for the pain Joab had experienced? Either way, Israel won, but David's trust in Joab was shaken. This story is so very complex; relationships can be risky business. Joab and David are proof of that.

A few years back, I needed to replace the water heater in my house. It was beyond my ability, so I asked an older gentleman for help. He seemed like "spiritual dad" material to me, so I was excited to spend time with him. That morning started pretty rough. On the way to the home improvement store, we both drank coffee. His was black; mine had cream and sugar. He let me know that "real men" drink black coffee. He then called my favorite mug a "sissy cup" and berated me for drinking my too-sweet coffee from it. I tried to laugh, but he was serious.

The whole experience of replacing the water heater was more abusive than it was instructive. Instead of patiently teaching, he doled out a lot of criticism for the knowledge I did not have. I remember arguing at one point about the amount of Teflon tape we were putting on a joint. I thought it was not enough, but he insisted it was. There was no compromising, so I let it go. Later that night, I fixed the joint that was already leaking by putting more Teflon tape on it. I appreciated the help and could not have done it without him. But the real reward of the experience was forfeited because there was no genuine desire to mentor. I had put myself out there, and I got hurt as a result. My new water heater hardly seemed worth it.

Maybe you are shying away from the kind of relationships I have been writing about because of experiences like the one I just described. Maybe your trust level is low, and your self-protection fence is high. I would never belittle your pain and would never tell you not to be cautious. Still, the reward of being mentored is worth the risk of being hurt. You can keep helping others. We all can do better. We can turn the tide and make mentorship the gift God intended it to be.

MENTORING MENTORS

In one of my leadership teachings, I use the bullseye of a large round archery target as an illustration of the highest goal of a disciple. The word *disciple* is used 270 times in the Bible. We should all want to be faithful disciples of Jesus. In my illustration, I keep jamming arrows into the target but not on the bullseye. I said each of the following sentences for every arrow jammed into the target.

> You may read the Bible daily, which is phenomenal, but it is not the bullseye of discipleship.
>
> Maybe your prayer life is next level, and that is one of the best things ever, but you still are not hitting dead center when it comes to being a disciple.
>
> You may tithe and serve and give to the poor, and all those things are incredible, but you still have not scored a direct hit.

No, the bullseye of discipleship is replication. True discipleship is when your faith is replicated in someone else. Disciples produce disciples.

The primary goal of mentorship is discipleship—when the traits of following Jesus that are active in you begin to grow in the person you are mentoring. Real mentorship is when someone gets close enough to see the work of Jesus in you. Mentorship is a contact sport—it takes proximity to make it work. When others get close, they will not be a perfect picture. We are all works in progress. We are all portraits of grace. You must be willing to be seen, or what is in you will never be modeled by someone else. Replication demands an example.

You know your mentorship has been effective when your mentee begins to mentor others. The greatest joy and highest reward a mentor can experience is seeing what you have taught being taught to someone else. Effective mentors live beyond themselves and establish a legacy for the blessing of future generations.

I love Paul's words in 1 Corinthians 11:1 (NIV): *"Follow my example, as I follow the example of Christ."* This sentiment is so different from what I hear from most men. I often hear, "Don't follow me. Don't look to me. I will let you down. Look to Jesus and only follow Him." Paul knew that people needed flesh-and-blood examples to look to as they lived for Jesus. Paul was a mentor.

We are told to *"teach these truths to other trustworthy people who will be able to pass them on to others"* (2 Timothy 2:2). What a cool concept. Mentors raise up mentors. When you teach someone what God has taught you, and you instruct them to teach others, you are assured that you will live beyond yourself. This is how the kingdom advances. This is how we multiply our impact.

FORGOTTEN LESSONS

Growing up, one of my favorite activities with my dad was fishing. We always struggled to find good places until Dad finally bought a boat. Then, we were off to the lake almost every weekend when the weather was right. His favorite kind of fish to go after was white bass. They are a smaller version of striped bass, and in the warmer months, they travel in schools. They are hard fighters; we could catch hundreds on the right days. It was an absolute blast.

One of the lessons Dad taught me was that when schools of white bass are feeding, they like to push shad onto sunken islands where the water is shallow. Locating these islands was challenging using our old depth finders. Our only hope was to gain insider knowledge of visual and underwater markers that could guide us to the hottest spots. We spent many early mornings watching our bass boat's archaic flashing sonar screen. Dad taught me to line up with towers and trees and read the fluctuations in depth that would lead us to the fish. I tried my best to remember what he showed me, but, to this day, I don't think I could find those islands without his help.

The problem with most of us is that we tend to forget the lessons we should remember. We can be mentored morning after morning, but if we don't intentionally make ourselves memorize what we are taught, we will soon forget it. God wants us to have an abundant life, but He is not obligated to remind us of everything we should have learned.

Scripture implores us:

Do not let kindness and truth leave you. Tie them around your neck. Write them upon your heart.

(Proverbs 3:3 NLV)

Mentorship only works when it is remembered.

One of the last times we see Joab in David's life is during an event that never should have happened. This is one of the most sobering stories in the Bible. For some reason, the aged king decides he needs to census Israel. Be careful not to measure your success as if it is your own.

David commands Joab to *"take a census of all the tribes of Israel—from Dan in the north to Beersheba in the south—so I may know how many people there are"* (2 Samuel 24:2). Joab immediately knows that this was wrong, and he gives the king a stern warning. He is once again a mighty mentor. *"Joab replied to the king, 'May the LORD your God let you live to see a hundred times as many people as there are now! But why, my lord the king, do you want to do this?'"* (2 Samuel 24:3).

In the next verse, we see David suffering from memory loss. He decides to ignore the very voice that had saved him years earlier. The king insists that Joab and his commanders take the census. (See 2 Samuel 24:4.) They come back with numbers, and David returns to his senses, but it is too late. David knows he has sinned and begins to beg for God's forgiveness. (See 2 Samuel 24:10.) God sends a plague as a judgment upon Israel, and 70,000 people die. The plague stops only when David purchases a special place and offers sacrifices to the Lord. (See 2 Samuel 24:18–25.) The king refused to heed Joab's advice, which cost him and Israel dearly.

Seeds planted are only as good as the soil they are received in. Your dad can show you the sunken treasures of a lake, but it is up to you to remember what you learned. So do whatever you must: journal, meet often, and ask your mentor to reshare a lesson. Tattoo it on your chest if you have to—but do not forget. Treat the time you get with those wiser than you as a precious gift. Create a special "lock box" in your memory for the things you learn. When the temptations and attacks of life come—and they will—you want to know where your best defenses are hidden. You want to remember what your mentors taught you.

9

ELITE FORCES
(DAVID & THE THIRTY-THREE)

> *So the Three broke through the Philistine lines, drew some water from the well by the gate in Bethlehem, and brought it back to David. But he refused to drink it. Instead, he poured it out as an offering to the Lord.*
> —2 Samuel 23:16

About twenty-five years ago, I had an opportunity to travel to the Philippines for two weeks and preach in evangelistic gatherings. These were a series of meetings in different locations with crowds of around a thousand or more. An evangelist friend was about to do major gatherings there and needed someone to speak at smaller outreaches that would set up his larger events. It was a phenomenal but exhausting opportunity.

After traveling around the Philippines for almost two weeks, I boarded a long flight to Los Angeles. Then I got on a red-eye headed home to Florida. As the plane took off, everyone settled in and tried to sleep—everyone, that is, except me. My internal clock was still eight hours behind on "Filipino time," and I was wide awake.

After an hour, a flight attendant approached me and said I was the only passenger not sleeping. She then surprised me with an offer to move up to first class! I gladly accepted, and I was served an excellent meal within minutes. Another flight attendant asked me, "What movie would you like to watch?" Back then, they played DVDs through an in-flight system with drop-down screens. I chose a movie that looked like a Western and was soon enthralled by the film. This movie spoke to me deeply. I can't remember the title, but I vividly recall the story.

The movie opens with a scene at the end of the Civil War. Quickly, they introduce a Confederate general who has been mortally wounded. In this long opening scene, viewers are invited into the dying general's tent, where he takes a large treasure map and spreads it over his desk. He meticulously rips the map into four equal pieces without saying a word. Then, one by one, he calls in four young soldiers. You can tell that he is a father figure or mentor to each of them. He individually tells each of the young men about a vast treasure and gives them each an equal piece of the torn map. Then, before he can introduce them to one another, he dies. Their prosperous futures are now connected to their potential friendship with each other. To be rich, they will first have to be in relationship.

The next quarter of the movie follows the four soldiers as they attempt to locate each other after the war. When they finally find the last piece of the map and assemble the map, it leads them to a treasure beyond their wildest dreams. Then, of course, robbers appear out of nowhere, trying to steal the treasure. The opposition unites the men around their mutual cause, and they become warriors for one another. They defend what has been given to them. In the struggle, a fusion of friendship happens that only men who have fought together can understand. They become brothers.

What I loved the most about the movie was that no one became jealous or greedy. Modern movies are so dark, and the characters are so jaded that you do not know for whom to cheer. These men refuse to ruin the gift they have been given with selfishness or greed. When individual egos rise, a noble mission turns into a cheap mercenary pursuit. The cause gets polluted and diluted until it is unrecognizable. These four soldiers defeated their foes without losing themselves in the process.

I love it when movies give you the "extra information" your soul longs to see. This one does not give one of those "artistic" self-interpretation endings that leave you guessing—I despise that! Instead, they show the men buying a ranch together and raising their families together. The general had given them a gift far more significant than money. He gifted them with the rare fortune of camaraderie and even family. They were no longer alone. They were on a mission together.

When I finished watching the movie, our plane was about halfway to its destination, giving me a few remaining hours of the flight to reflect on what I had just watched. I was so moved that I began to write in my journal about the power of people coming together for a cause. Some of the things God gave me that night became the foundational seeds for our nonprofit organization, which has facilitated hundreds of short-term mission trips. One of the lines I wrote that night was: "If we are going to find the treasure, we have to come together." This is true for all men. None of us alone holds all the pieces of our treasure map.

This "treasure map principle" is on display throughout David's life. The map of his life was divided into many key relational pieces. We find this most beautifully laid out in the astounding account of David's mighty men. In 2 Samuel 23, we are given a record of an elite force and a few remarkable details of their individual victories. These men are often compared to our modern-day special forces divisions like the Navy SEALs or the army's Delta Force. That analogy is solid, but it is not deep enough. These men did not enter David's inner circle simply because of training, skill, or mental toughness. Their status as elite warriors was based on loyalty and dedication to David, which separated them from the rest. These warriors loved their king.

This select list of men in 2 Samuel 23 is often called the "30 and the 3," even though the final verse of the chapter says, "*There were thirty-seven in all*" (2 Samuel 23:39). Scripture breaks down this fierce group of fighters into categories: a special "three" are singled out by their superior deeds and unparalleled loyalty to David; then, there are the leaders of the three and the thirty. Finally, there is a list of named soldiers and their tribes that forever separates them from the average masses. These thirty-seven men were chosen from the thousands of others who served. To make this list was a badge of honor, an earned right of the few.

Most of the people in David's life were attached to his calling. Some made only minor contributions, but many were key characters who were integral to his story. They were part of the inner circle that helped carry the massive weight of David's assignment. Every man requires a support system of elite forces who can help him reach new heights in life—men who inspire that man to realize his full potential because they possess a level of excellence that is both uncommon and rare. David could not have won the wars he was called to fight all by himself. He needed mighty men who had the same warrior spirit he did.

You have probably heard it said, "If you are the smartest person in the room, you are in the wrong room." This quote is attributed to many different people. A lot of people say it, but very few live it. Great people were drawn to David, but one of his consistent leadership traits was his lack of personal intimidation when surrounded by them. Many men allow their insecurities to limit the quality of their relationships. They must shine brighter than anyone else. They like being the superstar on a team of average players. David fought against the common smallness we see in men of power. The list of mighty men proves that he wanted and needed others to be elite in his kingdom.

ATTRACTIVE GREATNESS

Two of my favorite things about Jesus are how He prioritized being alone with His Father and the way He was around people. This wonderful relational duality was not a tension He managed but a passion He embraced—one actually caused the other. The more time Jesus spent with His Father, the more He loved people. The more He loved people, the more He needed to be alone with His Father. David possessed this same trait. He was known for his love of solitude but was also incredibly social. Most Christian men are one or the other, but the rare ones are both.

David had two "spiritual hothouses" in his life. The first was very simple and had only enough room for him and God. The accelerated growth on display in David's life happened because he spent countless hours in the perfect environment of God's

EVERY MAN REQUIRES A SUPPORT SYSTEM OF ELITE FORCES WHO CAN HELP HIM REACH NEW HEIGHTS IN LIFE—MEN WHO INSPIRE THAT MAN TO REALIZE HIS FULL POTENTIAL BECAUSE THEY POSSESS A LEVEL OF EXCELLENCE THAT IS BOTH UNCOMMON AND RARE.

presence. This secret place was the secret to his greatness. The second was much larger, as it represented his relationships with other people. This expansive place of growth was an exquisite jungle filled with beauty and danger. An abundance of fruits was produced here, but these fruits grew alongside thorns. David relationally navigated both the perilous and the purposeful because, like ours, his destiny was interwoven with his relationships. The mighty men were some of the most extraordinary relational accomplishments of David's life.

Some men may read about relationships like these and think, "I will never have people of that caliber in my life." Maybe you have been dogged by this doubt in every chapter. You think your life is not worthy of divine alliances like the ones David had. That nagging sentiment is wrong on multiple levels, but I will not deny that some men seem to have a "draw" to them that others struggle to create. David possessed an attractive greatness that made other warriors want to be with him. The question we modern men face is not one of worthiness but attractiveness. How can we attract the right people into our fight? How can we increase our chances of creating meaningful relationships with the elite forces God has for us?

I see five attractive leadership qualities in the epic historical events we are told about in 2 Samuel 23. Each of these qualities is illustrated by a courageous act on the part of one of David's mighty men.

THE WARRIOR MENTALITY

Proverbs 23:7 says, "*As he* [a man] *thinketh in his heart, so is he*" (KJV). It is your mentality that creates your reality. Your mind has the power to trap you where you are or move you toward where you're supposed to be. Men who think like a warrior eventually become one. I see this clearly in Jashobeam the Hacmonite, the first mighty man we are told about. Scripture says he *"was leader of the Three—the three mightiest warriors among David's men. He once used his spear to kill 800 enemy warriors in a single battle"* (2 Samuel 23:8).

Look at that kill number again: 800 in a single battle. That is astonishing. The best action films of all time cannot compete with Jashobeam! I looked it up, and the entire *Rambo* movie franchise only has John Rambo at just over 500 kills. There are actually stats available that record how many Rambo killed with his shirt on versus his shirt off! Some people have too much time on their hands! Can you imagine how Jashobeam felt as guy number 697 fell to his sword? He had to have thought, "No man could stand against me because God is with me." Warriors have a mentality of faith; they know they cannot lose if God is on their side. Who would not want to hang out with someone who thought like Jashobeam?

A REFUSAL TO GIVE UP

Warriors stay on the battlefield when everyone else runs the other way. Second Samuel 23:9–10 says, *"Next in rank among the Three was Eleazar son of Dodai, a descendant of Ahoah. Once Eleazar and David stood together against the Philistines when the entire Israelite army had fled. He killed Philistines until his hand was too tired to lift his sword."* No one is drawn to a quitter. If you want other warriors in your life, then you must stay in the fight. Resilience is relational fuel. Everybody wants to be around a man who endures.

FIGHTING FOR THE LITTLE THINGS

We see this trait in a warrior named Shammah. Second Samuel 23:11–12 says, "*One time the Philistines gathered at Lehi and attacked the Israelites in a field full of lentils. The Israelite army fled, but Shammah held his ground in the middle of the field and beat back the Philistines. So the LORD brought about a great victory.*" The Philistine army showed up in a field of lentils, and the Israelite army fled, but Shammah would not retreat. He found an opportunity to fight back amid a field of small yet nutritious legumes. Shammah literally fought for his food.

The problem with giving up a lentil field to the enemy is he never stops there. First, he takes your ability to use crops to make food, and then he wants more. The enemy will take as much territory as we let him have. Shammah fought for something small so the enemy could not try for something bigger. Where do you take your stand? Nothing is more attractive than a man who fights for the little things. People often notice the impressive big towers constructed by men, but those in elite circles focus on the essential foundations. The little disciplines no one seems to notice make a true warrior. In contrast, it is small compromises that ultimately destroy a man. Elite men fight for lentil fields.

BEING A LEADER OF LEADERS

I am willing to invest in anyone, but most of my energy goes toward those with leadership potential. When you invest in a leader, your investment is multiplied generationally. Jesus Himself did this. He loved thousands, but He spent the bulk of His time on earth with twelve men in whom He saw excellent leadership potential. Second Samuel 23:18 tells us, "*Abishai son of Zeruiah, the brother of Joab, was the leader of the Thirty.*" He also had great victories, some of which I wrote about in chapter five. His greatest quality was being a leader of leaders. One effective way to bring elite people into your life is to train them yourself. Leaders lead leaders.

ACTING ON FAITH AND RUNNING TOWARD RISK

My favorite character among the thirty-seven men is Benaiah. He was a *"valiant man"* and a *"doer of great deeds"* (2 Samuel 23:20 ESV). James, the brother of Jesus, wrote, *"As the body without the spirit is dead, so faith without deeds is dead"* (James 2:26 NIV). Most men talk a good game of faith, but real warriors are the ones who are moved to action. Benaiah was an active man of faith, and everyone wanted to connect with someone like that.

The latter part of verse 20 says that Benaiah killed *"two champions of Moab."* The Moabites were warriors who trained from birth. They were fierce and formidable. Benaiah took out their two best fighters. Then we hear of this random act of valor: *"Another time, on a snowy day, he chased a lion down into a pit and killed it"* (2 Samuel 23:20). People don't typically chase lions into pits, but Benaiah did. Who would not want to hear the details of that encounter? Elite people are doers, taking action and sharing their compelling stories. I have discovered that my strongest friendships have formed through shared elite experiences. Friendships are often formed around the retelling of the crazy battles we have fought. Men are drawn to stories. Taking risks of faith gives us something to talk about.

These principles are not a fast track to relational richness. In contrast, they produce long journeys that will lead to the best of traveling companions. Elite men draw elite men. In becoming leaders, we will find our inner circle, our warrior tribe. Be willing to develop these traits alone, if necessary, but you will not be alone for long. Warriors tend to discover others who share their mindset and actions. Your elite force will be revealed on the battlefields you are summoned to. This is what happened to David. His mighty men found him as he fought the battles he was called to fight.

MIGHTY MOTIVATION

Reviewing all these impossible victories has made me more aware of my inner and outer wars. These men were excited to enter the arena and fight, but I can't always say the same. Can you? It made me wonder: What motivated the mighty men? You cannot read these accounts without remarking at the seemingly endless supply of motivational passion in these guys. They certainly lived in a violent time, and courage was required of them in a more literal sense than it is of most of us today. Their days were dangerous, but their dedication was deeper than their desire to survive or even the appeal of the rewards of victory. These men had something we all need. These men deeply loved their king.

The mightiest motivation in the mighty men was their love for King David. They all served beyond what was required by their positions or even demanded by their country. They seemed to want success for David more than they wanted it for themselves. What transforms a great warrior into an elite one is a deep love for the leader they serve. Those who possess this love are willing to go beyond what seems rational and to push themselves further than others might consider possible.

This is another "type" coming from the story of David that imitates our own personal relationships with Jesus. We are called to love King Jesus passionately! Like many of you, I am in a royal romance with my Savior, and it drives me to be the best warrior I can be for Him. Giving my best for Jesus requires that I abandon the world's logic and rely on God's wisdom. Other men may call me crazy for my faith, but my passionate love for Jesus is my motivation.

A unique moment is relayed in 2 Samuel 23:15–17. Right in the middle of all the radical heroics is a story about the three mightiest men helping the king quench his thirst. Second Samuel 23:15 says, *"David remarked longingly to his men, 'Oh, how I would love some of that good water from the well by the gate in Bethlehem.'"* This is not the king giving an order. David is just being nostalgic and thinking about the best water he has ever consumed. It was from his hometown, but the Philistines had conquered that territory. To drink from that well would be a suicide mission, and no water is worth that kind of risk.

Verse 16 says, *"So the Three broke through the Philistine lines, drew some water from the well by the gate in Bethlehem, and brought it back to David."* David's three best warriors overhear what the king says and take it upon themselves to get him the water he desires. They go way beyond the call of duty. They will not let their king's thirst go unquenched.

I can only imagine how that mission planning session went!

"Did you hear that our king is thirsty?"

"No king of mine is going to be thirsty. Let's do it. Let's get him a drink."

Heads are nodding in agreement, and chests are bumped. They must be sneaky, but encounters with the enemy were inevitable. Eventually, the three elite warriors return to camp carrying the much-needed refreshment. They can't wait to satisfy the desire of their king.

Their gesture moves David so much that he refuses to drink the precious water and instead pours out as an offering to the Lord. (See verses 16–17.) The passage ends by saying, "*These are examples of the exploits of the Three*" (verse 17). In other words, these elite warriors were loyal and loved their king enough to perform even menial tasks of getting water for him. Motivation matters. Elite men have elite motivation. This is why we are drawn to passion and humility when we see it. Elite behavior is not self-identified. When your motivations are pure, others will count you among the elite.

TRIBE BUILDING

The most intimidating part of this passage might be the sheer number of mighty men in David's elite force. I mean, thirty-seven men of this caliber committed themselves to him. That does not count the plethora of relationships we have already discussed. David excelled in relationships at a level that very few can match.

Most of us would feel blessed if we could have just one covenant friendship or spiritual dad in our lifetime, let alone spend time with prophets or have a band of warriors to follow us around. Most of us just cannot imagine the type of relational air that David is breathing. Maybe that is where you are today. You can't compete with David. You could never pad the account of your relationship history with an elaborate list of elite men who fought by your side! Your tribe is small, and you think it will always be.

I will admit that I am intimidated, as well. To think of even beginning to approach thirty-seven elite men whom I could do life with is a daunting proposal. So, let's change the rules! If you don't like the game, then change the rules. We don't have

GIVING MY BEST FOR JESUS
REQUIRES THAT I ABANDON THE
WORLD'S LOGIC AND RELY ON
GOD'S WISDOM.

to lower the standard; we'll just change the way we approach the subject. Let's find a way to win.

Most of us do not have the capacity or the contacts for thirty-seven (or more) real-time high-caliber relationships. But we do have both the relational bandwidth and the network for some. Beyond that, we can get creative with time and space. In other words, we can have both "real-time" and what I will call "spiritually creative" elite relationships. We can make our tribe bigger by inviting elite people into it—even people we do not personally know.

We do this by committing to being personally discipled by anyone whose voice can be trusted, even if you do not have a personal relationship with that person. Did you know you are probably already practicing what I am talking about? Most of you reading this book are not personally connected to me. I would love to know you, but time and space limit us. The good news is, we are not letting that stop us! The miracle of writing or even watching one of the small-group videos is that what God put in me for you can travel across time and space. I can help you even if I do not know you.

I have received stories of my last book being read in prison cells that I could never access. It has been in countries I have never visited. My words have found themselves in the personal struggle of thousands of people whom I have never had the honor of meeting. This is the power of reading. You can be discipled by anyone who took the time to write.

So, should we be pursuing relationships at all? Absolutely! Nothing is better than the real thing. But this does not mean we can't connect in other ways. The limitations of this earth will always be something we have to work around.

Here are four ways to make your relational world bigger—even if you do not have the connections to make it happen.

OBSERVE ELITE LEADERS FROM AFAR

There are leaders whom I may never have the privilege to meet who have impacted my life significantly. They possess qualities that I admire and want to emulate. I haven't studied why they are the way they are, but their traits are easy to observe. Just the other day, I was so challenged by the humility I saw in one of the pastors I had a chance to speak for. This person didn't give me a specific charge; it was what I saw that still convicts me and moves me toward change. Anyone can do this! You do not have to have personal access to know greatness when you see it.

SIT UNDER THE LEADERSHIP OF A HIGH-END LEADER

This could be as simple as joining a men's Bible study led by a man you trust. It might be as simple as making a renewed commitment to never miss church and to sit under the quality teaching of your pastor. Maybe you work for someone who could take you to another level if you truly submitted to their leadership. This is as much about the posture of your heart as it is about your physical attendance. Most men are missing their biggest chances to be discipled because those chances are hiding in plain sight. The men are in attendance but not truly present. God puts elite people in your life for a reason—you must take advantage of it.

READ AND STUDY

You may not be the best student, but everyone has some capacity to learn. Your pace may not be as fast as others', but most men have the ability to read the written word. Becoming a better reader is another opportunity to invite a mentor into your life. Few things will change your world and increase the pace of your growth as much as reading. If you want to be a leader, you must become a reader. Charles Spurgeon has taught me discipleship. He is one of the best writers I have ever read. He passed away many years ago, yet he remains one of the elite influences in my life because I value studying. Your relational circle grows exponentially when you develop the heart of a student.

PURSUE ELITE RELATIONSHIPS

I have found that many of the elite men in my life are there because I intentionally asked them to be my friends. In other cases, they're the ones who asked me. A few years ago, an elite leader approached me after speaking at a conference in Idaho and asked if I had time for lunch. I agreed, and the next day, we sat in a restaurant talking for four hours. He is now a dear friend and a part of my elite force of relationships that are taking me to a new level. I've received way more from him than I have been asked to give. Most men lack the courage to ask. Be Spirit-led, graceful, and selective, but, by all means, have the courage to ask. Then, practice honor and never overwhelm anyone. Respect the time you get with men who can take you to another level.

God does not play favorites. He loved David, but He loves you just as much. David may have been a king, but he needed lots of help, just as you do. Your Father does not care less for your needs because your kingdom may be smaller than David's was. God wants you to be surrounded by warriors who can help you become the complete man He knows you can be. He has elite things for you to do, so He will be faithful in providing the elite people you need. Get creative, but never compromise. You need to find your tribe. Every man does.

NEVER FORGOTTEN

The final man mentioned in this amazing list may surprise you. He is someone I'm sure David would have liked to forget. He is a person who represents the lowest moment in David's reign. He is a reminder of failure, but he is also a reminder of God's grace. His name is *"Uriah the Hittite"* (2 Samuel 23:39). He was Bathsheba's husband, the man whose death in battle David had arranged by ordering that the army pull back from him in the heat of the fighting. (See 2 Samuel 11:15.) He was married to the woman with whom David committed adultery. Yep, this guy is the one the king would like to forget. Yet, when the Holy Spirit is inspiring Scripture, Uriah gets a last-second add to one of the most prestigious lists in the Bible. He gets to be remembered as a mighty man.

One of our biggest mental hangups when discussing high-end relationships is our fear of being forgotten. Most of us have been "ghosted" so many times that we have developed scar tissue from all the relational wounds. Our fear of being forgotten can create a caution that makes us tentative with everyone. The only way to battle this fear is to know that Jesus never leaves a man behind. He never forgets us. He remembers His mighty men even when they are victimized by a king.

In my Bible reading, I often review the story of Joseph being imprisoned for a crime he did not commit. (See Genesis 39–40.) While in prison, he helps Pharaoh chief cupbearer by interpreting a dream of his. The cupbearer promises to remember him once he is freed from prison. Instead, he *"forgot all about Joseph, never giving him another thought"* (Genesis 40:23). I have been there, and so have you. Someone promised to invest in your freedom, but they forgot you instead. These situations hurt, and the disappointment tends to linger.

I want you to hear me again on this. Men may forget you, but God never will. Men may want a "clean record" that you are not a part of, but God will remember to put your name where it belongs. Joseph still made his way out of prison and to the palace. Everyone still heard about a great warrior named Uriah. God remembers Uriah and Joseph because they are His. You are His, too. So, trust in the most elite force a man will ever encounter. Trust in the faithfulness of your God. He is the one writing your relational story. Refuse to get stuck in your loneliest chapters. God never forgets mighty men.

10

GOD'S HEART
(BECOMING A MAN WHO CHASES
THE HEART OF GOD)

> *The LORD has sought out a man after his own heart.*
> *The LORD has already appointed him to be*
> *the leader of his people.*
> —1 Samuel 13:14

Before we even meet David, we already know the most important thing about him. We know he is a chaser of the heart of God. We know that God has been watching him before we could see him. God saw humility. God saw courage. God saw a heart that would obey Him. In this chapter, we will go back to the beginning. We will look at the foundational relationship of David's life—his relationship with God's heart. This is the very definition of who David was. He was a *"man after my* [God's] *own heart"* (Acts 13:22).

We all have a reputation that precedes us, something we are defined by. Every man is known by his character traits. Sometimes, we oversimplify things by saying, for example, "He's a really good guy, or maybe, "That dude is always angry." We are all known for something. David was known for his relentless pursuit of the heart of God. What an amazing thing to be known for! Nothing could be greater. This is the first and best thing we learn about David. His love for God made the "soil" of his life fertile ground where relationships could flourish. David made relationships with people look effortless because he had established his relationship with God first. Every man, regardless of personality type, can do this. You can excel in this area, but you must know God's heart first.

Few things in life are more powerful than being chosen. We all remember standing in line waiting to be picked for a kickball team or that dreaded dodgeball game. The cool "captains" surveyed the crowd, and all you could do was wait and hope you weren't picked last. Everybody wants to be chosen. This is one of those involuntary spiritual and emotional traits we all have. From the time we are children, we crave to be selected and assigned. We all want to be wanted. This desire in our souls is a whisper of the divine. God put in us the need to be chosen. God also created in us the ability and free will to choose Him. His desire is for us to choose Him as He has chosen us. Even God loves being chosen.

In Psalm 78, we read this about David:

> [God] *chose his servant David, calling him from the sheep pens. He took David from tending the ewes and lambs and*

made him the shepherd of Jacob's descendants—God's own people, Israel. He cared for them with a true heart and led them with skillful hands. (Psalm 78:70–72)

God chose David. He searched for a man who loved His heart and found one in David. In Psalm 89:19–20, He says, *"I have raised up a warrior. I have selected him from the common people to be king. I have found my servant David. I have anointed him with my holy oil."* The Message translation puts it this way: *"I've crowned a hero, I chose the best I could find; I found David"* (Psalm 89:19 MSG).

First Samuel 13:14 tells us that God *"sought out a man after his own heart."* God is always seeking men who are after His heart. This should speak loudly to anyone who feels trapped in obscurity. You may think you are hidden, but if you seek God's heart, He will find you. This is how God chooses. His radar is always searching, and it only has one setting: "Purity of Heart." Second Chronicles 16:9 (AMP) tells us, *"The eyes of the LORD move to and fro throughout the earth so that He may support those whose heart is completely His."* Our God is a searcher. He loves searching for people who want to give Him their hearts entirely. No shepherd field is remote enough to keep God from finding a man seeking after Him.

In John 15:16 (AMP), Jesus declares, *"You have not chosen Me, but I have chosen you and I have appointed and placed and purposefully planted you, so that you would go and bear fruit and keep on bearing, and that your fruit will remain and be lasting."* You are not where you are by accident. God has purposefully *"planted you"* and placed the right people around you. You have been chosen. You have been appointed to *"bear fruit"* that will last beyond you.

OUR GOD IS A SEARCHER. HE LOVES SEARCHING FOR PEOPLE WHO WANT TO GIVE HIM THEIR HEARTS ENTIRELY.

spirit, and I wrote exactly what He said in my journal. I rarely share entries from my journal, but I want to share this one with you. God said to me:

> Stop trying to get noticed. Refuse to angle, position, or manipulate. I have a plan for you that cannot be forced into existence—it has to unfold in its season. Obedience is what produces opportunity. Rest. Obey. Rest in your obedience. Everything else will take care of itself.

Are you "resting in your obedience," or are you trying to angle, position, and manipulate? That is a powerful question for any man who wants God's heart to be the driving force of his life. Forced success leaves a bad taste in your mouth. Miracles cannot be manipulated. Perfect positioning in God's kingdom is not about getting everything you want. It is about seeking His heart and letting Him find you. His promotions are always for your good. His ways of positioning you where you need to be are always perfect.

SPECIAL UTENSILS

Plastic has become a highly controversial topic lately. While most people acknowledge that this incredible material has improved our lives, there is concern about its environmental impact. Through my travels worldwide, I have come to agree that we can and should do better. Billions of plastic utensils are used yearly, and some regions have even outlawed single-use plastics.

Did you know that the Bible has a strong opinion on the subject of utensils? The apostle Paul weighs in on the matter in his second letter to Timothy, his *"son in the faith"* (1 Timothy 1:2):

Fruitfulness in the kingdom of God is always a relational proposition. Being fruitful signifies that your relationship with God and others is elevating to another level. Knowing God's heart will produce so much fruit that even nations could be blessed through you. This is what God did for David and what He wants to do for us: make us fruitful.

POSITIONED PERFECTION

In my younger days, I played a lot of basketball. I had a pretty good outside shot, but because I am tall, I often found myself guarding bigger guys under the basket. Positioning is increasingly crucial the closer players get to the basket. When a player is in the correct position, he can make comfortable moves, significantly increasing his chances of scoring. However, if you can keep him off balance and out of position, making a shot becomes much more challenging. This is why physicality increases in the "paint" near the basket. Elbows are thrown, bodies are pushed, and tempers can flare when someone is out of position.

Decades ago, as a youth pastor, I played on a basketball team in a local church league. One particular night, we were getting scored on regularly by a big center dominating in the paint. No one could stop him. The coach had me playing on the perimeter, but I asked if I could guard the big center who was giving us so many problems. The more I studied him, the more I was convinced that he had only one move. He would fake to the left and then do a drop step in the opposite direction. This move gave him the perfect position for his little hook shot. I thought that if I could wait for the fake and then stop in the middle of where he wanted to go, it would frustrate his game. My defensive strategy worked like a charm. He lost his position and became so enraged at his inability to score that he lost his temper and actually started throwing punches! No one likes being out of position.

The average eye would not have looked at young David and thought he was in the correct position to be promoted by God. He was from the wrong family, lacked the proper training, and had a very undesirable job. Even within his own family, David was not positioned for anything but more monotony. However, God looks at things differently than we do. Man evaluates by logic and appearance, but God looks at the heart. (See 1 Samuel 16:7). David's obsession with the heart of God put him in the perfect position to be blessed by God. This is why things sometimes seemed so easy for David. When you are correctly positioned, it is not hard to "run up the score" on the enemy. All the power and opportunity one could ever need are freely given to the man whose heart is properly positioned before God.

Earlier in the book, we discussed David's refusal to promote himself. This was perhaps David's most admirable trait. His "positioned perfection" had to come from God, or David would not want it. This is opposite of the way most men operate today. The natural tendency is to force your way into the "scoring position," even if you have to throw a few elbows to clear the court. That is no way to catch God's heart. We never have to fight for position when we put Him in charge of our destinies.

Many years ago, I was in a season of feeling limited and desiring more opportunities. I was dissatisfied with what I had received, and my ambition overwhelmed me. My heart was discontent, divided, and just plain bored. I even started making some small attempts at self-promotion, thinking I could self-generate some success. Then, one morning in prayer, the Holy Spirit began to deal with me. He clearly spoke to my

> *In a wealthy home some utensils are made of gold and silver, and some are made of wood and clay. The expensive utensils are used for special occasions, and the cheap ones are for everyday use. If you keep yourself pure, you will be a special utensil for honorable use. Your life will be clean, and you will be ready for the Master to use you for every good work.* (2 Timothy 2:20–21)

Paul separates the priceless china from something you can pick up in a discount store. He speaks about special gold and silver, the kind of stuff your grandmother has that she brings out only on special occasions or for important guests. Paul says you can be ordinary, like the plastic cup you kept the last time you were at a ball game. Or you can be extraordinary, like the precious stemware your grandfather brought back from his business trip to Paris. You can live your life like you are cheap plastic designed for onetime use, or you can be set apart for the special purposes of God.

You are not plastic. God did not design you to be used a couple of times and then thrown away. You are supposed to be used by God repeatedly. What makes the difference? How can you be a *"special utensil"*? Paul says, *"If you keep yourself pure,"* you will be set apart for special use by the Master. If you keep yourself clean, God will use you for *"every good work."* You will have many good things coming out of your life. Your purity will raise your potential higher than you ever thought it could go. This is what God did for David. He raised his potential because He saw his purity.

Paul goes on to tell Timothy to *"run from anything that stimulates youthful lusts. Instead, pursue righteous living, faithfulness, love, and peace. Enjoy the companionship of those who call on the

Lord with pure hearts" (2 Timothy 2:22). Men know precisely what Paul is talking about. We have become so inundated by lustful things that it seems almost impossible to avoid them. Pornography is so pervasive now that many men have stopped running from it. Maybe that is your struggle. Perhaps you have accepted the unacceptable because it has often defeated you. I say this with great compassion: get back in the fight. You cannot pursue lust and pursue Jesus at the same time. God has better things for you than the cheap imitations of intimacy offered by this world. Your lack of purity will steal your potential if you let it.

I love that Paul gets relational in the latter part of the verse. He says, *"Enjoy the companionship of those who call on the Lord with pure hearts."* Cut off relationships that draw you away from God and seek out men who pursue Him as you do. Pure hearts are attracted to other pure hearts. Purity is a battle that cannot be won alone; you need companions to fight alongside you. Special utensils never sit alone in a drawer or mix with everyday items. They belong with others like them, thriving when used together. This is what God wants for you. This is how we keep our hearts pure.

HEART THERMOMETERS

David was a writer. He was a master craftsman, and words were the tools he used to express his heart. We know that David wrote more than seventy psalms, and some scholars believe he wrote many more. One of the reasons we know David's heart so well is that we can read his words. Words are the way the heart tells us about itself. If you get around someone with a bitter heart, it won't be long until you hear bitter words. In the same way, pure hearts will not sit in silence forever. The heart will

GOD HAS BETTER THINGS FOR YOU THAN THE CHEAP IMITATIONS OF INTIMACY OFFERED BY THIS WORLD. YOUR LACK OF PURITY WILL STEAL YOUR POTENTIAL IF YOU LET IT.

eventually speak. The way you measure the condition of your heart is to listen to your words. Words are the thermometer of your heart.

When a doctor takes your temperature, it helps him evaluate your condition. He uses that information to determine if you are well or sick. When we are spiritually sick, it manifests itself in in the *temperature* of our speech. Jesus said, *"Out of the abundance of the heart [a person's] mouth speaks"* (Luke 6:45 NKJV). In another place, He said, *"Whatever is in your **heart** determines what you **say**"* (Matthew 12:34). Jesus also used this analogy: *"A tree is identified by its fruit. If a tree is good, its fruit will be good. If a tree is bad, its fruit will be bad"* (Matthew 12:33). The *"fruit"* of a person's life is identified by what they verbalize. Our tongues are *"a flame of fire"* (James 3:6). We must be on guard; a man's speech is his dead giveaway—let him talk, and he will show you his heart.

I found the following principle true after conducting interviews for positions with our organization: let a person speak, and they will tell you who they are. God gave us one mouth and two ears for a reason. I try to listen more than I speak when getting to know someone. Jesus took this truth even further in Matthew 15, when He was confronted by religious leaders about whether or not eating unclean food can defile the soul. Instead of confirming their legalistic views, Jesus confronted them about the power of their words, saying, *"The words you speak come from the heart—that's what **defiles you**"* (Matthew 15:18). He then gave them a list of the many sins that result from speaking evil. (See Matthew 15:19–20.) Jesus connected behavior with speech. He told them that their hypocrisy was a result of their evil words.

I have a bag of dry grass seed in my garage. If I poured water on it, the seeds would sprout in a few days, even without soil. That's because water activates growth. Similarly, verbalizing negative thoughts can lead to fulfilling those desires, as expressing a willingness brings it closer to reality. Your words are an activator. The way you talk will eventually transform the way you act. Being careful with our words is vital because we always want to activate the right seeds. A sinful word spoken can result in a life broken. Someone who just read that sentence needs to commit themselves to a season of silence. You need to hush until you are healed. Speak when your heart is right again, but not before then.

Maybe this is why God so often sent David into lonely caves. He knew that David needed solitude, time alone with Him, before He could give voice to his calling. Public communication is complex to take back, especially today. Wisdom would keep us in the caves longer, so when we speak, our words are a product of time alone with Jesus. This is the only kind of speech that changes the world. God wants to change how we talk, but we must know His heart first.

In Psalm 139, David uses his words to express what kind of man he wants to be.

> *Search me [thoroughly], O God, and know my heart; test me and know my anxious thoughts; and see if there is any wicked or hurtful way in me, and lead me in the everlasting way.* (Psalm 139:23–24 AMP)

David is asking God to navigate the mystery of his heart.

Just as our physical heart is hidden in our chest, our spiritual heart is also hidden. Jeremiah wrote, "*The heart is deceitful above all things, and desperately wicked; who can know it?*" (Jeremiah

17:9 NKJV). The heart is a maze of contradictions with so many twists and turns that we will surely get lost if we explore it on our own. Only God can truly search our hearts.

HEART HEALTH

How is your heart doing? You might need a checkup. Do you want a heart like David's but find yourself unsure of where to start? Here are three steps toward better heart health:

YOU MUST BE CAREFUL WHAT YOU CONSUME.

Heart patients know they cannot eat whatever they want and have a healthy heart. Your heart is impacted by what you watch and listen to. You cannot out-pray a lousy diet. Consume the good things of God. Your consumption affects the way you function.

YOU MUST DECIDE THAT YOU WILL MONITOR YOUR WORDS.

The way I do this is with journaling. I write down my struggles about what I say and ask God to correct it. Most men lack verbal awareness. Pay attention to your speech, and it will accelerate your spiritual growth. This will also give you an accurate way of measuring your progress.

YOU MUST IMPROVE YOUR COMMUNICATION WITH RELATIONAL ACCOUNTABILITY.

Other people often understand what we say more clearly than we do ourselves. Surround yourself with trusted individuals who will hold you accountable for your words. Consider praying with someone about the spiritual ramifications of your words. Negative words can reveal an unforgiving or entitled heart. Fatalistic speech can indicate a lack of trust in God.

Cursing can show you that sin is still lurking in your heart. Allow your friends to discuss your speech with you. This is how we come to understand our hearts.

David's greatest weapon was not his sling or his sword. His most powerful armament was his ability to articulate his faith in God. He waged wars with his words. We see this clearly in both his encounters and his writing. He spoke faith to Goliath before he ever slung a rock at him. (See 1 Samuel 17:45–47.) Journalist Edward R. Murrow said of Winston Churchill as he refused to make concessions to Hitler during World War II, "He mobilized the English language and sent it into battle."[22] This is what all of David's songs are about. It was his warrior heart giving voice to the faith inside of him. Every man should weaponize his speech in the direction of his faith. Say the words. Express your love and confidence in Jesus. It is good for your heart.

SURVIVAL INSTINCTS

In my last book, I revealed my love of survival TV shows. It is an obsession of mine that goes beyond the sixty-five-inch screen in my living room. I love reading about survival and learning from anyone who has done it. I even love looking at all the products to help with survival, like fire starters and temporary shelters. Perhaps, one day, I will truly be lost in a wilderness, and all this knowledge will be put to good use!

One of the things I've learned about survival is a meaningful mantra to help someone find civilization when they are lost in the wild. It goes like this: "Creeks lead to streams, streams lead to rivers, and rivers lead to towns." Why are towns important? Because there are people there. Rivers represent abundance.

---

22. "Photos of Winston Churchill at War," HistoryNet, accessed January 9, 2025, https://www.historynet.com/photos-of-winston-churchill-at-war/winston.

This is why we build towns next to them. People gather by rivers because there are resources there. Rivers bring commerce, and they open lanes of travel. You are connected to the world when you are near a river. It is hard to be lonely when you live by a waterway.

Jesus once used the concept of rivers as an analogy for what happens to a man when he knows Him.

> *If any man is thirsty, let him come to Me and drink! He who believes in Me [who cleaves to and trusts in and relies on Me] as the Scripture has said, from his innermost being shall flow [continuously] springs and* **rivers** *of living water.*
> (John 7:37–38 AMPC)

I was sixteen when I was introduced to Jesus and believed in His great love for me. I took a drink of the salvation He offered. He forgave me and filled me with His Spirit. That day, the river began to flow, and it did not stop. My relationship with Him has only become deeper and stronger.

What I've found in my own life is that loving Jesus has led me to people. The stream of His love has become a raging river, and that flow has led me to many rich relationships. When you encounter Jesus, you cannot remain lost in the wilderness you once were. You have to get to the river, which will always lead you to people.

If I had never met Jesus, most of the places where we do mission work would never have made it onto the map of my life. My calling would never have taken me to the places for which I now have such great affection. Meeting Jesus connected me with my dear partners and many precious people I never would have encountered otherwise. I even met my wife because of my walk with Jesus. The river of His love has caused a flood of rich relationships.

Jesus called Himself *"living water"* (John 4:10) and He said we should drink of Him so that we might never be thirsty again. (See verse 14.) Drinking the *"living water"* Jesus offers means your endless thirst is finally quenched. You can help others and have something eternally valuable to share. You are no longer just trying to survive. You can move to a town and begin to thrive. You can be relational like Jesus was. You can invite people into your world that you had no room for before. You can even go places you had no reason to go to before. Now, you have something to offer. Now, you have a reason to be relational. You don't have to be lonely anymore.

David quenched his spiritual thirst by drinking in the presence of God.

> *The one thing I ask of the LORD—the thing I seek most— is to live in the house of the LORD all the days of my life, delighting in the LORD's perfections and meditating in his Temple.* (Psalm 27:4)

This warrior-king could not get enough time with his God. He quenched his thirst for God regularly. In Psalm 63:1, he cries, *"O God, you are my God; I earnestly search for you. My soul thirsts for you; my whole body longs for you in this parched and weary land where there is no water."* This is why David had so much love to give. He satisfied his thirst by seeking God. If you want to improve your human relationships, spend time in God's presence.

I find it amazing that even though David was trying to survive, he still thrived relationally. The future king hid in caves, but men wouldn't stop gathering at his side. (See 1 Chronicles

12.) The Bible tells us that David's ranks swelled several times. *"All these were fighting men who volunteered to serve in the ranks. They came to Hebron fully determined to make David king over all Israel"* (1 Chronicles 12:38 NIV). David's close relationship with God brought him a profound river of favor with others. It is hard to believe that all this started in the lonely shepherd's fields outside of Bethlehem—but it did. David's relationship secret was time alone with his heavenly Father. His heart for God is what created his heart for people.

GUARDED GLORY

Security teams are a relatively new part of church life. Only in the last couple of decades have we felt the need to have active protection as a part of our Sunday morning experience. I am thankful every time I speak at a church that has this area covered. I have had a few encounters where security has been really helpful. Plus, there is just something comforting about knowing you are guarded. Feeling safe is never a bad thing.

I was recently speaking at a church that had assigned a couple of security guys in suits to follow me around. I thought it was overkill, especially since they were so serious. To lighten the mood, I turned to one of them and said, "You know, if necessary, I am willing to sacrifice both of your lives to save my own, but I will tell your story everywhere I go." I laughed, but they didn't. Instead, I got a determined nod from both of them! Nobody was going to mess with me that day. I was covered.

The thing we must guard above all else is the glory of God. We have to protect His glory from both ourselves and others. We never want to take the credit that only belongs to God. Nothing offends the heart of God more than someone pridefully taking for themselves the praise that only belongs to Him.

Stealing God's glory was King Saul's great sin. He even built a monument to himself to get some credit for God's victories. (See 1 Samuel 15:12.) This is part of the reason God took the kingdom from him and gave it to David. God gave the kingdom to someone who would respect and protect His glory.

One of the first occasions that reveals David's his desire to glorify God is in his speech to Goliath. David told the giant that he came in the name of the Lord. (See 1 Samuel 17:45.) He described how Goliath would die and even what David would do with his body. This was some incredible trash talk from the young shepherd! He then revealed his genuine heart and shared his desire to glorify God:

> The whole world will know that there is a God in Israel. All those gathered here will know that it is not by sword or spear that the Lord saves; for the battle is the Lord's, and he will give all of you into our hands. (1 Samuel 17:46–47 NIV)

He was basically saying, "Goliath, you are going down. But not so I can be famous. A shepherd boy is going to kill you so God can receive even more fame." David wanted to make his God famous.

Do you want the whole world to know about your God? Do you want Him to be known, or do you want yourself to be known? You must choose in your heart. God selected David because he could trust David with His glory. It is important to note that God chose a worshipping warrior to be king. Worshippers know how to give God glory.

You may not be the songwriter that David was. You may not play the harp well enough to drive away depression, but you can be a passionate worshipper of God. This is essential if you want to be a man after God's own heart, like David was.

Worshippers guard the glory. Worshippers know who put them on the throne. Worshippers give God all the credit He deserves.

What a relational quality this is. An unwillingness to take the credit you do not deserve is something we all strive for. I like to say that credit is poison. It's the "hot potato" that you should want to pass along. David's most attractive quality might have been his refusal to take credit for the things God had done. This trait created favor between God and man. David's desire to glorify God caused God to trust him. His world got bigger because his ego remained small. Humility opens doors. Relationships naturally flow toward a man with a humble heart.

CONCLUSION: THE PERFECT TEN MYTH

Let us consider [thoughtfully] how we may encourage one another to love and to do good deeds.
—Hebrews 10:24 (AMP)

We moved to a new state a few years ago and purchased a home. Our area's inventory of homes was very limited, so our only real choice was new construction. As we were moving in, our builder warned us that we should expect some encounters with bugs, snakes, and maybe other critters because our lot had been cut out of the forest just a few years earlier. Now that we had built and "disturbed the land," we could expect a few run-ins with the local creatures. He said, "They don't know that this is not their home anymore." He was right. It is much better now, but during the first couple of years, we caught about twenty small snakes in the sticky traps we kept in our garage. Running off all the unwelcome guests from our little piece of land took a while.

As we have taken this relationship journey together, the "land" has been disturbed. You and I are beginning the "new construction" of our bigger, better relational homes. These new residences may or may not be as large and palatial as one of King David's residences, but they will be ours, and we will thrive there. Mark it down today: the enemy does not want you to succeed in relationships. He still thinks his old lies and established insecurities should rule your land. You have to trap and kill every one of them, like we did to the snakes in our garage. Keep up the battle until they know better than to come back. Kick every last unwelcome guest off your property. This is your incredible new home, and it is time to live there.

When God called David out of the shepherd fields, there was no way he could have known what to expect. There was a throne in his future, but there was also a madman king who would make it his mission to kill him. There would be hundreds of deep and rich friendships, but there would also be more battles than he could count. A web of complications would replace the simplicity of David's shepherd-boy existence. David was called to take the ground that was already occupied. No wonder he ran into so much opposition.

The relational life God wants to give you is contested territory. Healthy relationships are a spiritual thing that gets the attention of spiritual forces. The most well-known passage about spiritual warfare in the Bible is Ephesians 6, where Paul tells us that *"our struggle is not against flesh and blood, but against the rulers, against the authorities, against the powers of this dark* world and against the spiritual forces of evil in the heavenly realms" (Ephesians 6:12 NIV). It may not surprise you that nine instructional verses on relationships precede Paul's famous seven verses on spiritual warfare in Ephesians 6. When you get better with people, it gets the enemy's attention every time. You can expect a fight when you disturb ground that he thinks is his.

PERFECTION PERSONIFIED

The only perfect relationship you will ever have is your relationship with Jesus. He is perfectly faithful. Second Timothy 2:13 says, *"If we are unfaithful, he remains faithful, for he cannot deny who he is."* Jesus is so faithful because His faithfulness doesn't depend on us. He bases His faithfulness on His character, not ours. Relational perfection is only possible with Jesus. There may be struggles, and it may get messy, but in the end, His faithfulness will win the day. Psalm 33:4 (NIV) says, *"He is faithful in all he does."* On some level, everyone and everything will eventually let you down, but He never will.

One of our biggest problems with relationships is our efforts to place a standard of perfection on something that is inherently flawed. No human relationship can accurately personify the perfection we can only have with Jesus. We cannot demand of people something only God can give. But we do, don't we? In our minds, we begin relational journeys with so much expectation that we will inevitably be disappointed. Sometimes, we do this on purpose so we are sure to sabotage the relationship before we get hurt. We create "fables" and "legends" in our memories about "perfect" relationships from days gone by. This way, no one can live up to our standards. People are flawed. You are flawed. Perfect relationships are a myth.

As I wrote this book, I was well aware of the radical standards I was setting. I mean, who has all of these different relationships in their life? David is such an outlier that we will never have another example like him. Plus, we are taking his entire adult life as a study, but we are just mere men struggling in the moment. We cannot compare our current realities to David's lifetime of relationships.

David's biblical example has to be translated into our lives by an intimate work of the Holy Spirit. You are not David, and neither am I. However, we can learn from the man Scripture tells us so much about. We can all strive to be relational men. We can get better together.

MASTERING MYTHS

There are three basic myths I want to unveil. These are the three myths of the "perfect ten":

MYTH 1: ALL RELATIONSHIPS ARE FOR ALL SEASONS

No one will have all ten of these relationship categories active simultaneously. We do not need a "brave prophet" every day. The "Nathans" God sends to us will be vital but rare. My "spiritual fathers" were critical for much of my life, but in the last few years, my focus has been on raising "spiritual sons." A "covenant friendship" or a "mighty mentor" can be overtaxed if they are called upon too often. Thank God that "ordained opposition" is not my daily reality. Those people are seasonal and necessary, but they are never permanent fixtures in my daily existence. The "perfect ten" is a myth we must put in its place. The goal is to have the right relationships at the right time.

MYTH 2: *GOD ONLY USES PEOPLE I GET ALONG WITH*

I talked a lot about this in chapters two and eight. God will not always send us the people we want, but He will send the people we need. We must embrace this truth or rob ourselves of many crucial relationships. In my life, I am careful not to remove every "abrasive" person I encounter. Some of my best friendships took years of struggle to develop. Sometimes, God will put a person in your path who sees life differently than you do. This could be your greatest chance to grow. This lowest form of relationship is mutual agreement. The highest form is a mutual challenge. Challenging people are necessary if you want to be the man God calls you to be.

MYTH 3: *RELATIONSHIPS ARE SUPPOSED TO ENDURE*

We live in a temporary world—things are always ending and beginning. People are constantly growing and changing. Some people change for the better, and some regress. Sometimes, your growth outpaces your friendships. In heaven, our capacity to manage relationships will be significantly expanded. But for now, we must be acutely aware that most of our relationships will not endure for a lifetime. This does not mean you have to keep score and officially break things off with anyone. It does mean that you must follow Jesus closely and be willing to let people go.

COMMITTED CREATIVITY

Is there a greater mission than the one discussed in this book? If you think about it, Jesus died for the cause of relationships. His death made your relationship with God possible. It meant that you could be redeemed, forgiven, and healed. His sacrifice opened the pathway that led to your transformation.

This means that not only can you have a healthy relationship with God, but you can have healthy relationships with people, too. Before I met Jesus, all my relationships were affected by my brokenness. I just used people to get what I needed. Jesus is the one who taught me how to love. Because He first loved me, I learned how to love others.

The writer of Hebrews must have been a relational guy. Hebrews 10:24 provides some excellent relationship advice. *"Let us consider [thoughtfully] how we may encourage one another to love and to do good deeds"* (Hebrews 10:24 AMP). *The Message* translation of this verse reads, *"Let's see how inventive we can be in encouraging."* The Bible says that we should get creative with our encouragement! We should invent ways to encourage each other. I think God is calling some inventors to step forward and start a movement that creates ways to get men together. He wants us to get creative in our approach to developing relationships.

The very next verse in Hebrews 10 takes it even deeper: *"Let us not neglect our meeting together, as some people do, but encourage one another, especially now that the day of his return is drawing near"* (Hebrews 10:25). We are told to get even more committed to meeting together as we get closer to the end. We will need each other even more when the heat gets turned up. We must not neglect this command. We must be relational men.

So, today, I call you out of your loneliness. I declare that you are needed and wanted. You are not meant to do life alone. Your very destiny is intertwined with the destinies of other godly men. You are built for relationships. Your calling is too important and too significant to live out by yourself. You may be hidden in a cave now, but others will be drawn to you. If you chase God's heart in your obscurity, He will make your world bigger. The quality of your comrades will increase as your character grows. You are a connected man. You are a kingdom person. God has great people with whom you can live life. God has rich relationships in store for you.

ABOUT THE AUTHOR

Doug K. Reed is a full-time writer and speaker who travels to conferences and churches in the U.S. and internationally. He is the president of Partnership International, a nonprofit organization dedicated to completing meaningful mission projects in some of the world's poorest environments. Partnership International has hosted thousands of people on short-term mission trips with the goal of completing meaningful construction projects for the neediest among us.

Doug also has more than thirty years of ministry experience and has served in several positions in the local church, including that of lead pastor. He is currently a teaching pastor at three churches—in Kansas City, Missouri; Chester, Virginia; and Troy, Missouri.

He and his wife reside in the Tri-Cities area south of Richmond, Virginia.

For more information about Partnership International, visit www.pitrips.com. For more information about Doug, visit www.dougkreed.com.